Walking With God lets us see who we are—and where we are going.

"The truth of the whole matter is that when we are born into the family of God anew, we are endowed with a capacity to see; to understand clearly what our Father is like . . . . We can see the direction in which He is taking us. We can find out what our destination will be."

Walking With God "is for the common man on the common road. It is for the weary and worn who have lost their way and are uncertain where to turn. It is for the eager ones, anxious to get on the high road to wholesome living. It is intended especially for seeking souls who long to walk with God in humble joy—who ache fiercely for the Master's friendship."

BY W. Phillip Keller

W. Phillip Keller

WALKING
WITH
GOD

***Power
Books***

FLEMING H. REVELL COMPANY

Old Tappan, New Jersey

Unless otherwise identified, Scripture quotations in this volume are from the King James Version of the Bible.

Scripture quotations identified WEYMOUTH are from WEYMOUTH'S NEW TESTAMENT IN MODERN SPEECH by Richard Francis Weymouth. Published by special arrangement with James Clarke & Company, Ltd., and reprinted by permission of Harper & Row, Publishers, Inc.

Scripture quotations identified PHILLIPS are from THE NEW TESTAMENT IN MODERN ENGLISH (Revised Edition), translated by J. B. Phillips. © J. B. Phillips 1958, 1960, 1972. Used by permission of Macmillan Publishing Co., Inc.

Library of Congress Cataloging in Publication Data
Keller, Weldon Phillip, date
Walking with God.
1. Christian life—1960–   I. Title.
BV4501.2.K426   248.4   80-16431
ISBN 0-8007-5187-6

TO
WAYFARERS
WHO
WISH TO WALK WITH GOD
AND
ENJOY HIM AS THEIR FRIEND

Contents

He hath shewed thee, O man,
What is good; and what doth
The Lord require of thee,
But to do justly, and to love mercy,
And to walk humbly with thy God?

MICAH 6:8

A Word of Thanks

This is to express genuine gratitude to my home church for inviting me to give this series of lectures during their Sunday services.

A special note of appreciation goes to my friend Rene Chamberland, who made such a fine job of the tapes which were put at my disposal.

I am thankful for the care and accuracy of the typing done by my wife, Ursula. She becomes ever more proficient at reading my difficult handwritten manuscripts.

I am grateful to Ernie Owen, editorial director at Fleming H. Revell Company. He suggested such a book several years ago. Then he was willing to wait patiently for it to come to life.

Finally I am humbly thankful to the Lord, for His presence, so real and manifest, directing me in the writing.

W. PHILLIP KELLER

The Theme of This Book

Two thrilling themes traverse the timeless truth of God's Word. They run like a parallel set of footprints across the sacred pages of Scripture. They are imprints left upon the sands of human history by God and man.

The first theme clearly shows us the generous, gracious, loving steps God Himself has taken. From out the splendor and magnificence of His heavenly realm the Self-giving, Self-sharing Saviour has come to descend to the depths of our dilemma to deliver us. Strongly, surely, He, the eternal, the magnificent One, has lived, moved, and suffered amongst us. By coming to walk with us, to talk with us, to suffer in our stead, He has delivered us from despair to love; from darkness to light; from death to life.

Not only has He shown Himself to be our God, our Saviour, our Father, but also our Friend.

As such, He, in turn, invites us to come and walk with Him. That is the second theme, the essence and message of this little book.

All through the ages, God has extended a warm welcome to wayfaring men to join Him. He has extended His hand to any who would turn toward Him. He has opened His great heart to any who cared to come to Him. He joyously invites us to join Him on the path of life. He calls us to joyous days and His own highways. There is new terrain waiting to be explored, new horizons to reach, new heights to climb in His company.

Walking with God can be exhilarating. It can be fulfilling. It can be downright delightful. He is a wondrous traveling companion. He does not, of course, guarantee only fair weather. There will be some stormy spells as well. But in His company the trip can be a triumph.

In recent years millions of people claim to have been "born again." Almost as many say they have been filled with God's Spirit—yet many have not yet learned to go on and walk with God in harmony. I pray these pages will provide help in that direction.

This book is not a deep doctrinal discussion of difficult subjects. It is not intended for those who are already great scholars of the Scripture. It is for the common man on the common road. It is for the weary and worn who have lost their way and are uncertain where to turn. It is for the eager ones, anxious to get on the high road to wholesome living. It is intended especially for those seeking souls who long to walk with God in humble joy—who ache fiercely for the Master's friendship.

For purposes of clarity and simplicity, I have deliberately chosen to write in layman's language. Yet some of the chapters deal with profound spiritual truths that may have bewildered the reader before. My most earnest hope and prayers are that because of this book, bright light from God's own gracious presence will fall not only upon the pages but also upon the path the reader walks henceforth.

To enlarge and enhance the reader's understanding of

what it really means to walk with God, the whole theme has been handled from the whole of life. This is not some sophisticated spiritual thesis. It is the practical application of God's own divine principles to every area of our spirits, souls, and bodies.

We are called to walk with Him in wholeness; in wholesomeness; in holiness. No pains have been spared to make it abundantly obvious that no matter what our culture, society, or time in history, He invites us to walk with Him in dignity, decency, and on a plain above and apart from our contemporaries.

It is a thrilling theme. It calls us to the loftiest levels. Christ challenges us to great conquests and quiet contentment. His Spirit is eager to share the trail with us. God waits, smiling, eager to be a Friend, as we walk together.

Come, let us go!

"Walking Together With God" (What It Means)

The Background

The phrase *Walking with God* is not just a picturesque piece of spiritual sentiment. It is not a mere bit of poetic rhetoric. It is not an empty expression of wishful thinking.

Rather, it can be the powerful, pulsing principle that permeates all of life. It can be the central concept that directs and determines a devout life in company with Christ. It can be the daily delight of the man or woman who loves and knows God. It can be the sharing of our journey with His Spirit.

We can walk together with God. We can share life with Him. We can be acutely aware of His presence on the path. We can know His intimate friendship. We can be guided by Him in every area we enter. We can sense His gracious Spirit by our side, speaking distinctly, emphatically saying to us, "This is the way; walk in it."

This is the life to which God calls human beings. He longs for our companionship. Down across the long centuries of human history, He has come and come and come, calling men and women to walk with Him. Some have responded in lofty, noble lives that set them apart from and above their contemporaries.

To name but a few, there was Enoch, my favorite hero of all heroes in the Scriptures. We are told emphatically that Enoch walked with God for three hundred years. Then he was not, for God called him "home" to Himself.

We are astonished at the incredible life of Abraham. Called from his native homeland, he set out across the desert wastes to walk with God in explicit faith. He stood beneath the desert stars and responded positively to the still, small voice of God's Spirit, assuring him of being the founder of a chosen, special people. He would be the father of a race through which "the Saviour" would come. And Abraham walked with God in that quiet, strong assurance.

We see men like Moses, Joshua, and Caleb who, despite the deviation of their contemporaries, chose to walk with God. Across the desolate desert wastes between Egypt and the land of promise, for forty years they kept company with God. A thousand frustrations with their fierce temptations to turn back from the path set before them could not deter them from walking with God.

In the retinue of the mighty men of faith and fortitude, we find Gideon, Samuel, David, Elijah, Elisha and Daniel. They knew God. They walked with Him. Together they trod the tough, testing trails of their times. Undaunted by the degradation all around them; living above the contamination of their culture; separated to God from the sinfulness of their society, they moved in mutual harmony with Him who had called them to walk with Him in wholeness.

We hear the prophets of old, men crying out to their contemporaries in clarion tones: "Come apart and be a separate, unique, special people." For the most part it was a cry that went unheeded. It was the voice shouting in the wilderness of men's despair, darkness, and degradation. Yet those who did respond found God. They found light. They found love. They found life. They found in Him a friend.

Then in fullness of time, God, very God, stepped upon the stage of human history in human guise. He, the Christ, came amongst us, lived amongst us, walked amongst us. From the generation of His day, Jesus called many to follow Him. At first more than eighty responded. Of these eventually only twelve remained. For three years they "walked with God," though scarcely knowing it.

What then does it *really* mean to walk with Him? What is implied by walking together with the Eternal One?

1) *Walking Together With God Means Harmony*

It is virtually impossible for two people to walk together, unless they are in agreement. You will notice that if there is the least discord, one or the other will quickly move ahead, while the other deliberately falls behind. They immediately separate.

Amos, the ancient prophet of old, called of God from caring for cattle to the lofty role of a prophet to his people, put it this way: "Can two walk together, except they be agreed?" (Amos 3:3).

So the sharp, stabbing, startling question comes to us. Are you in agreement with God? Are you in accord with Christ? Are you in sympathy with and sensitive to the overtures of His Spirit? Unless you are, to speak of walking with God is sheer self-delusion.

It is noteworthy that the people who walk together are those who are extremely fond of each other. Parent and child, sweethearts, lovers, chums, intimates, husbands and wives are the ones who have close and enduring bonds of harmony between them. There is a unique and special "oneness" which makes walking together a treat, a joy, a pleasure.

So it must be asked, is there harmony between you and God? Is He your favorite Friend? Are you in step with Him? Have you gotten into stride with His Spirit? Do you look forward eagerly to quiet interludes with the Master, with your Father in heaven?

2) *Walking Together With God Means Sharing*

In the opening pages of this book I made the remark that God has called to men across the centuries to come and walk with Him, because He wanted to share life with them. He had special insights and secrets to share.

Two people will not walk together, unless they have something in common to share. Parents and children, friends, lovers, business associates will walk with one another, often in close embrace, because there is something very personal, very private, very precious they wish to share.

So to be very practical and very honest it must be asked, is Christ your confidante? Do you, in a dilemma, turn to the telephone to call a friend or family member for counsel and encouragement? Or do you turn to God? Who is your closest intimate? Is it the Spirit of the Living Lord who resides with you?

If in truth, and not just in theory, we are walking together with God, we sense, know, and are acutely aware that He is our "alongside One." He is our companion, our counselor, our comrade on the path of life. It is to Him we turn always to share all the details and intimacies of our days.

3) *Walking Together With God Means Learning*

When two people go out to walk together, the main motivation at times is to learn what they can about each other. This in part explains why children and parents, lovers or sweethearts spend time strolling together. It is why an older man will take a young lad for a hike in the hills. It is the reason for business associates taking a walk together.

Walking in company with another, we communicate not only our knowledge and experience to our companions but, most important, our character—ourselves.

Our Lord invited men and women from every walk of life to come and join Him. There was something to learn. He said emphatically that if anyone became His child, His follower, His disciple, His companion, His student, if you wish, he would daily discover that he was learning to have His outlook, His attitudes, His approach to life.

Walking with Christ implies, therefore, that as I come to learn what His character really is I shall comply with His wishes and carry out His commands.

Do you know Him this well? Are you this familiar with His will? Have you learned that to love Him is to obey Him?

4) *Walking Together With God Means Exercise*

One of the great, wholesome benefits that comes from walking with a friend is the exercise it provides. And even though the trail may be steep at times, and the path rough and rocky, the interlude is a healthy, happy aid to our general well-being.

In this age of the automobile most of us do not walk nearly as much as we should for the benefit of our bodies. It is a splendid exercise and insures vigor and vitality.

Similarly, in walking with God we are called upon to exercise ourselves. We are invited to invest something of our strength and confidence in Him. To walk with God is to trust Him. To join Him in life's journey is to invest our faith in His leadership and direction of our affairs.

Far too many present-day Christians consider walking with God some sort of soft, sentimental sensation that panders purely to their feelings. We do not walk with God that way. We are pilgrims and wayfarers on the rugged road of a rocky, unregenerate world—and the only way to walk it with God is in unshakable faith in His capacity to accompany us and encourage us all the way. This takes faith in His character. It will exercise us to the utmost. It is what develops godly stamina.

The Word of God to us today is exactly the same as it was to Joshua long ago.

Only be thou strong and very courageous, that thou mayest observe to do according to all the law, which Moses my servant commanded thee: turn not from it to the right hand or to the left, that thou mayest prosper whithersoever thou goest.

This book of the law shall not depart out of thy mouth; but thou shalt meditate therein day and night, that thou mayest observe to do according to all that is written therein: for then thou shalt make thy way prosperous, and then thou shalt have good success.

Have not I commanded thee? Be strong and of a good courage; be not afraid, neither be thou dismayed: for the Lord thy God is with thee whithersoever thou goest.

Joshua 1:7-9

5) *Walking Together With God Means Separation*

It is obvious, is it not, that when two people go out to walk together, they automatically separate themselves—not only from their usual associates—but also from the same old familiar four walls of their homes?

There is something very refreshing, very beneficial in getting clear away from the same old, familiar surroundings into the fresh air, sunshine, and brisk breezes out-of-doors. It does us a world of good.

Christ calls us in the same special way. He called the fishermen from their familiar nets, boats, and beloved Lake of Galilee. He called Matthew from his tax collector's post. He called Mary from plying her "profession" as a prostitute.

God calls us to walk with Him away from the old garrulous gang; away from the cozy comfort of our conventional little circle of companions; away from the sometimes tired and worn-out, weary old world that has enclosed us and cramped us within its confines for so long.

Are you jaded with life? Is your little round of living a bore and a drag? God calls you to come out of it, get clear of it, break away from your old behavior patterns. Part company with your former companions who only contributed to your skepticism and cynicism. Leave the wretched old world with its hopeless ways and despairing days. Allow God's gracious Spirit to separate you from the staleness of a sinking society.

As of old, the call of God to us is:

> . . . I will dwell in them, and walk in them; and I will be their God, and they shall be my people. Wherefore come out from among them, and be ye separate, saith the Lord, and touch not the unclean thing; and I will

receive you, And will be a Father unto you, and ye shall
be my sons and daughters, saith the Lord Almighty.

2 Corinthians 6:16-18

6) *Walking Together With God Means Inspiration*

All my life I have been a keen walker, an enthusiastic
hiker, ardent mountain climber. Always associated with
these activities are the joy, exhilaration, and inspiration that
come from exploring new terrain. There is stupendous
pleasure in pushing back our horizons, getting a fresh
glimpse of new ground. The thrill of new views and wide
vistas over and across untrod territory is an exhilaration that
stirs the blood, quickens the pulse, arouses ambition. The
prompt response of every fiber in one's being is "Come
on—let's go!"

You will recall that over and over in God's record of His
dealings with men, He showed them new vistas of what they
could accomplish in His company. In ancient times He
called Abraham outside his tent to look at the stars. He took
Moses to gaze across the Jordan at the land of promise. He
communed with Elijah at the brook Cherith.

Do you know anything at all about being in such close
company, alone, with God, that He shares new vistas with
you? Have you been invigorated, inspired, enthused (*en
theo*—in God) by having Him open up before your won-
dering eyes worlds of possibility new and untrod yet by you?
Have you sensed His Spirit saying to you, "I will bless you
to the ends of the earth. I will enlarge your influence, extend
your impact to ten thousand lives as we walk together"?

God in Christ by His Spirit calls you to step out of despair
into the love of His life. He invites you to step out of darkness to walk in the brilliant sunlight of His presence and

person and power. Read 1 John chapter 1; it will do you good. It will inspire you to enjoy Christ in the light of His bright communion.

7) *Walking Together With God Means Going Places*

It is not enough to merely be shown sweeping new vistas and beckoning horizons. If a man or woman has any heart at all, he or she will head up the trail in full stride, determined to go places and take in fresh territory.

As God's people we are not armchair travelers. We do not walk by proxy. We set out to plant our feet on fresh ground. We set the soles of our boots on terrain they never tramped over before. We are on the move. Nothing will deter or divert us from our destination.

The blood-tingling, pulse-quickening assurance given by God to Joshua, as he stood on the banks of the Jordan, thirty-four hundred years ago, is exactly the same to us today. Gazing out across the land of Canaan, flowing with milk and honey, God declared emphatically:

> [Joshua] . . . go over this Jordan, thou, and all this people, unto the land which I do give to them, even to the children of Israel. Every place that the sole of your foot shall tread upon, that have I given unto you. . . .
>
> Joshua 1:2, 3

And Joshua did exactly what he had been told. He moved himself and a multitude of two million others with him across the Jordan and into the land promised to his people. Every step he took was an act of explicit confidence in God. He went places. He took territory. He walked in company with God.

Is this happening in your life? Are you moving onto new ground with God? Are you taking seriously the promptings of His Spirit? Are the commands of Christ a compulsion to you that cannot be contravened?

8) *Walking Together With God Means Climbing*

Anyone who does much walking or hiking soon discovers that much of its pleasure comes from the challenge of climbing. We are not content to just loaf along on the level: to dawdle in the lowlands becomes a bore. Something stirs within us to scale the heights; to tackle the ridges; to gain the summit; to get onto high ground.

It is precisely the same in walking together with God. Let me assure you that Christ is no ordinary hiking companion. He is not content to let you linger too long in the valleys of ease and lethargy. Instead, He calls us to a challenging walk. We don't dawdle in the ditch of despair or side roads of worldly skepticism.

There is far, far too often a tendency on the part of Christians, both amongst leaders and laypeople, to try and make their people feel comfortable, cozy, and contented in their padded pews. The church can become a community of emotional cripples, leaning upon each other for mutual comfort and consolation, without meeting the crying needs of a broken world all around.

Christ challenges us to go out and face the fury of the storm. He bids us climb the cliff and search the mountainside for the lost and straying. He compels us with His own compassion to accompany Him along the highways and hedgerows in search of stragglers and self-willed sinners.

We are called to noble service. We are drawn to part ways with the hedonistic culture of our times that indulges in and idolizes pleasure, leisure, and luxury. God calls us to walk with Him on the lofty level of self-sacrifice, self-giving, and self-sharing, that others be saved and salvaged for His dear sake.

9) *Walking Together With God Means Good News*

To have been anywhere in high country is to bring back good news of glorious days. The exciting adventures of the high country are amongst the most precious moments any man or woman can possess. They are gold bullion stored in the vaults of memory.

The Prophet Isaiah shouted this word to his own contemporaries:

How beautiful upon the mountains are the feet of him that bringeth good tidings, that publisheth peace; that bringeth good tidings of good, that publisheth salvation; that saith unto Zion, Thy God reigneth!

Isaiah 52:7

As we walk humbly with our Lord on the high road of holiness and wholesomeness, our lives make an impact for Him far beyond our most sanguine hopes. It is the man who firsthand knows what it is to walk quietly, intimately, serenely with Christ, whose life carries a special compulsion.

Not only does he bear a unique message of good news from God, but even his own life and conduct and character are an impersonation of that message. He knows God.

As with the disciples it was said: "They had been with Jesus." So it can be with you.

That is the theme of this book.

SECTION
I
WALKING WITH GOD
IN MY SPIRIT

CHAPTER

1
Walking With God
in My Intuition

God's Unique Revelation

The Word of God makes clear to us that man is a tripartite being. This is both a divine declaration and a spiritual revelation. By that is meant that it is not the view held by science or man in his unregenerate condition.

The Scriptures show that man has three distinct and separate realms to his makeup. They are *spirit, soul,* and *body.* These are closely interrelated. They interact in remarkable complexity; yet each has its own unique functions or capacities.

For purposes of simplicity and clarity, each of the three areas will be treated separately in this book. We will observe how we walk with God in our spirits, in our souls, and in our bodies. At the same time, it has to be borne in mind that the three are so closely intertwined that each exerts great influence upon the others.

Before we begin to do that, however, it is worth noting the special significance of the term *revelation* or *divine revelation* used at the beginning of this chapter. This so-called *revelation* is truth revealed to man by God about both Himself and man. It means God has thrown light upon subjects which could not otherwise be understood by us. In short, He has dispelled the darkness of our ignorance, both as to His own nature and ours.

Put in plain language, God in Christ, by His own gracious Spirit, shows us not only what He is like but also what we ourselves are like. It is a generous self-disclosure.

Of course many people react with great hostility to this exposure. When the illumination of God's truth, like a brilliant searchlight, floods over and lights up the sublime character of God and the sordid degradation of man in his sin, they shun it. They recoil from it. They prefer to delude themselves that it simply is not so. They declare vehemently that to accept such a revelation is folly.

There are two reasons for this. The first was stated very emphatically by our Lord when He declared:

> ... Light has come into the world, and men have loved the darkness rather than the Light, because their deeds have been wicked. For every wrongdoer hates the light, and does not come into it, for fear his actions should be exposed.
>
> John 3:19, 20
> WEYMOUTH

The second reason was given by Paul in writing to the worldly church at Corinth:

> ... Eye hath not seen, nor ear heard, neither have entered into the heart of man, the things which God hath prepared for them that love him.

But God hath revealed them unto us by his Spirit: for the Spirit searcheth all things, yea, the deep things of God.

1 Corinthians 2:9, 10

But the natural man receiveth not the things of the Spirit of God: for they are foolishness unto him: neither can he know them, because they are spiritually discerned.

1 Corinthians 2:14

In the light of these facts it can be seen why man has difficulty in accepting God's revelation. God's view of both Himself and ourselves is repudiated and rejected by the majority. It is not surprising, therefore, that the discussion of spiritual principles and concepts is often difficult, even amongst so-called Christians.

Compounding this problem is modern man's preoccupation with science and the so-called scientific process. It is based exclusively on observable phenomena which can be measured and recorded by one or more of our fallible five senses of sight, hearing, taste, touch, or smell.

But the things of the Spirit are not so measurable. And because they are outside of and beyond the scope of science, they are either ignored or treated with contempt—as if they did not exist.

The extreme absurdity of this can be seen when we pause to remind ourselves that such forces as love, faith, hope, and compassion, which are of the spirit, transcend all other values in life. But it does help to explain why, in part at least, the things of the Spirit receive so little attention in the

twentieth-century society of our Western world. That is
why, as a people, we are becoming impoverished in spirit.

God's Spirit Touches Our Intuition

In God's economy and in His estimation, the spirit is the
central citadel of life. Unlike the world and human society,
which endeavors to manipulate man through outside influences, God begins His deep and unique work within the
realm of our spirits. He touches us first at the very center of
our being in the realm of our spiritual intuition.

Spiritual intuition is the unique capacity given to man by
God Himself to know God. It is the amazing ability to be
acutely, intensely aware of God. It is the intense inner sensi-
tivity to the presence and person of God, in Christ, by His
Spirit. Spiritual intuition recognizes, "Oh, God, You are
here! I am in Your presence!"

The writer to the Hebrew Christians of the early church
put it this way:

> . . . he that cometh to God must believe
> that he is, and that he is a rewarder
> of them that diligently seek him.
>
> Hebrews 11:6

So, because God, who Himself is a Spirit, begins His initial overtures to us in our spirits, inviting us to walk with
Him in this realm, that is where I, too, choose to begin this
study.

But before proceeding further, the accompanying rough
outline is given to show the tripartite nature of man. Each of
these will be discussed in detail, showing how we walk with
God in that area of life.

INTUITION—The capacity to KNOW GOD.
SPIRIT CONSCIENCE—The capacity to SEE GOD.
COMMUNION—The capacity to Commune
WITH GOD.

MIND—The capacity to THINK: REASON:
LEARN.
SOUL EMOTIONS—The capacity to FEEL:
INTERACT WITH OTHERS.
WILL—The capacity to DECIDE: CHOOSE:
DETERMINE.

DRIVES—The capacity to EXERCISE
INSTINCTS.
BODY DESIRES—The capacity for APPETITES:
PASSIONS.
DAILY HABITS—The capacity for DAILY
CONDUCT.

The Nature of the Spirit

God Himself, our Lord told us, is a Spirit. And those who worship Him (commune and enjoy His company) must do so in spirit and truth (John 4:24). From this it follows that we, too, have the capacity to know Him in Spirit.

Spirit is not merely meaningless mysticism. So often the church and Christians are charged with indulging in spurious superstition. Spirit has substance. It has energy and influence. It has the capacity to accomplish and achieve great ends. Yet because it is above and beyond finite limitations it cannot be measured or manipulated by finite men.

Not only is God a Spirit but so also is Satan. The hosts of angels are ministering spirits ordained of God for special service. Demons are evil spirits. And every man has a spirit—which in most men is declared by God to be dead by virtue of the fact that it is not "alive" to God, or quickened (made alive) by response to the touch and influence of His own Spirit.

Jesus told the Jews very emphatically, "It is the Spirit which gives life. The flesh confers no benefit whatever. The words I have spoken to you are Spirit and are Life" (John 6:63 WEYMOUTH).

The Word of God reveals to us that spirit is capable of many activities that we can comprehend. It can perceive, understand, grieve, rejoice, decide, move, be fervent, be calm, worship, love and sing. But perhaps most important, we can know within the depths of our intuition in a way that far transcends "knowing," either in our souls (merely understanding with the mind), or bodies (sensing with our five physical senses).

What It Means to Know God in Spirit

Many dear people, with the very best of intentions, endeavor to know God with the faculty of their souls, by use of their minds or emotions or even their wills. They struggle to understand God. He cannot be comprehended that way. At best they end up knowing only about Him.

It is perfectly possible to spend the whole of one's life reading, studying, and discussing either a "historical God" or a "doctrinal God" or researching and seeking for "the historical Jesus" or "an ethical Jesus," yet never come to know Him either in spirit or in truth.

This was precisely the problem facing Nicodemus, the brilliant Old Testament scholar, steeped in the Scriptures, who was considered a master rabbi. He knew all about God, yet he had never come alive in his spirit to the Spirit of God. The eternal life of the Eternal God had never been allowed to quicken, energize and enliven his spirit. There had been no positive response, no interaction, no correspondence, no intercourse between God's Spirit and his dormant (dead) spirit.

Our Lord looked at the dear old Patriarch in love and compassionate longing:

> Oh, Nicodemus, that which is born of the flesh [soul and body] is flesh. That which is born [generated, activated, initiated], brought forth, and brought to life by God's Spirit is spirit. You simply must be born anew [in a new way; from above].
>
> *See* John 3:6, 7

In dismay and disbelief the pious old Pharisee looked at Jesus and shook his hoary head in perplexity. He did not understand. He did not know what the young Teacher was saying. The things of God's Spirit were utterly foreign to him.

"You mean to say you are a master in Israel and you don't know these things?" Jesus exclaimed in sorrow. "I'm simply telling you what I know and have seen" (*see* John 3:10, 11).

This "knowing" of which our Lord repeatedly spoke not only eluded and bewildered Nicodemus, but still does baffle most people. Even preachers, teachers, and lay people bandy about such phrases as "knowing God," "being born again," "walking in the Spirit"—without comprehending their enormous implications.

Often these ideas are simply pious-sounding phrases that are used to spread a veneer of superficial spirituality over a life that may be very much alive in other areas but is still very, very dead to God.

Quite obviously we have to be alive to God before we can walk with Him.

We have to know His life before we can move in Him.

We have to experience His energy before we can expend His energy.

We have to get something from God before we can use it.

We have to receive His life before we can live His life.

Let me explain. In the realm of my body I am said to be "alive" to my environment only so long as I derive my energy, sustenance, support and life from it. This I do by virtue of interaction with the natural world around me. There is said to be correspondence between me and all the physical elements surrounding me that contribute to my life.

I am surrounded by fresh air, sunshine, moisture, edible crops, warmth (heat), and minerals, all of which must be taken in daily to sustain and maintain life. I am said to be alive to them. I know them. I live and move and have my being in them.

If no such interaction or correspondence is carried on, if it ceases, I am then declared dead. I am said "not to know" anything anymore.

Precisely the same process is at work in the realm of my soul. On every side, I am surrounded by all the human accomplishments of society and culture. The influence of literature, tradition, learning, science, the arts, music, ethics, and social niceties are all about me.

I may be very much "alive" to these assorted influences. They may energize my mind, arouse my emotions, and move my will. They may quicken my soul and energize me mightily as I learn to know them, understand them, enter into them, and to love them.

But by precisely the same measure I may be "dead" to all

of this. The symphonies of Beethoven; the paintings of Rembrandt; the writings of Shakespeare may mean absolutely nothing to me. *I don't know them. I have no interaction. There is no intercourse. I am not alive to them. They do not stimulate, quicken, or energize my soul.*

So it is in coming to know God, to walk with Him in spirit. He surrounds me on every side with His own presence and person and power. Paul put it very bluntly to the skeptics at Athens. He said: "It is in Him that we move and live and have our very being" (*see* Acts 17:27, 28).

He is here. As we open our spirits to the gentle touch of His Spirit, we derive and draw spiritual sustenance from Him. He literally becomes our life. As we allow His Spirit to actually enter our spirits in quiet, still, receptivity, He does come in to share life with us (Revelation 3:20).

It is as we give time and opportunity and exposure of our spirits to Him that we become "alive" to Him. We have transmitted to us life of a caliber and a quality other than either physical (bodily) life or moral, intellectual (soulish) life. We actually are given the life of God—life from above—the eternal life of Christ Himself.

This is to know God. This is to be born anew in spirit.

New Life—Eternal, Everlasting Life

The instant an infant is delivered from the total darkness of its mother's warm womb, into the brilliant light of the wide new world around it, its life is drawn from a totally new environment. No longer is it dependent on the placenta that supplied it with nourishment from the body of its mother. It suddenly knows a new atmosphere.

If it is to survive it must immediately inhale great gulps of air from the atmosphere to which it is now exposed and which surrounds it on every side. In very truth it is in the air and the air must be in it (enter its lungs) or it will be declared by the doctor to be dead. If no correspondence is established with the oxygen around it, the child will never come alive to grow, walk, and mature into an adult.

God's revelation to us is that precisely the same principle applies in the realm of the spirit. The Scriptures speak clearly of God's people being delivered from the power of darkness (and our dependence on the bodily, fleshly, soulish life of our old mother earth), to be exposed to the new environment and kingdom of God Himself in His Son (Colossians 1:13).

It is a powerful parallel. No longer do we depend on the former life for our life. No longer do we live cramped and constricted in the darkness of our old life-style. We have been transferred into a new environment. We are delivered into a fresh atmosphere. It is an atmosphere alive, energized, charged with the wind of God's own gracious, generous Spirit. New, fresh air from God flows to us. His life engulfs, enfolds, surrounds, supports, and permeates us.

Jesus told Nicodemus this. He insisted that just as the wind comes and goes at will, blowing where it may, so the Spirit of God surrounds those born from above. He is there to vitalize and invigorate any human spirit that in-breathes and partakes of His presence. And those who do, experience, taste, *know* the in-rushing, sustaining life of the Eternal God.

And this is eternal life [everlasting life], to know Thee the only true God [Spirit], and Jesus Christ whom Thou hast sent.

John 17:3 WEYMOUTH

As long as there is mutual correspondence; mutual awareness; mutual interchange; mutual receptivity between God's Spirit and my spirit, I experience, know, and have spiritual life . . . Christ's life . . . God's life . . . ongoing, eternal life.

In other words He is the very environment of my spiritual intuition. It is in Him, from Him, by Him that I derive all spiritual support, sustenance and strength. This is why Paul stated so simply yet profoundly: *"For me to live is Christ!"* For this giant, in God's economy the supreme attainment was to *know God in Christ by his spirit.* (Read Philippians 3:4–14.)

The Quality of This New Life

It simply is not good enough for a man or woman to claim that they have been "born again," or "born anew" or "born from above," without there being the accompanying evidence of such a new life. It is pious fraud to claim one has the eternal life of God, if there are no signs to support the assertion.

A newborn infant very soon lets the whole world know in unmistakable terms that it has new life in its new environment. Very much alive, it breathes deeply. It cries and calls out. It develops an enormous appetite that demands frequent feedings. It gurgles contentedly in the comfort and reassurance of its family. It rests and sleeps soundly. It moves its legs and arms, rolls about, and soon tries to learn how to walk.

We look for the same signs in a newborn child of God. His inspiration (in-breathing) should start to come from God. He should be willing to give voice and witness to the

new life within, vigorously, vehemently. A keen appetite
and hunger should develop for the milk of God's Word. The
Scriptures should become a new and strengthening source of
stamina—something that is drawn upon eagerly, daily.
There should be a sense of gaiety and joy and contentment
in the company and fellowship of God's family. There
should be quiet rest in God. By degrees we should see the
newborn one exercising faith, beginning to try and take the
first faltering steps to walk with God.

If these simple signs are missing, we have every reason to
question the authenticity of the claim to being "born again,"
of *knowing God,* or having eternal life in fellowship with *His
Spirit.*

The church is full of "stillborn" babes. There may have
been a time of delivery. But the new life came to nothing.
There has been no "aliveness," no "growth," no walking
with God, no maturing.

The "born again" person soon discovers that if he or she
is in Christ, old things (former things) are passed away. All
things become new and changed because of the process of
re-creation that goes on in the presence of and under the im-
pulse of God's Word and God's Spirit (2 Corinthians 5:17).

The daily diet of feeding on God's Word; the steady exposure to His Spirit in that Word, in prayer, in quiet meditation, in compliance with His commands, brings about enormous changes in the newborn Christian.

The old worldly ways; the flashy, fleshly life-style; the old,
loose standards of morality; the self-indulgence, selfish self-
interest; the duplicity and deception; the rivalry, bitterness,
and hostility all begin to be patterns of the past. In their
place the wind of God's Spirit and the presence of Christ's
person bring about goodwill; good cheer; honesty; compas-

sion; self-sharing; wholesomeness; integrity; purity and decency.

God's Spirit touches man's spirit. It blossoms into new
life. It bears a distinct quality of goodness, wholeness, and
joy. There is peace and contentment. The Spirit of God
communes with the spirit of man, stating clearly, "This is
the way, walk in it. It is the way everlasting, it is life eternal
to know Me and walk with Me!"

2
Walking With God
in a Good Conscience

Harmony With God

In the opening pages of this book it was made very clear that for two people to walk together happily there must be harmony. Likewise in our relationship to our Heavenly Father there must be a clear, unclouded, uncluttered companionship as we walk through life together.

We simply have to see in a very simple way, not only what He is like; what His interests are; but also where He is going. Far too many Christians have the curious notion that it really is not possible to truly know God. They think rather naively that they must more or less follow Christ in blind faith. They are often led to believe very wrongly that there is no way in which they can possibly know where God is likely to lead them. They are hopelessly in the dark as to what intentions their Father in heaven may have for them.

All of this is absurd.

It is in fact a reprehensible reflection on God Himself.

It is as if to say He really does not know how to lead us in open, bright, joyful companionship where together we can walk life's road in bright light.

The truth of the whole matter is that when we are born into the family of God anew, we are endowed with a capacity to see; to understand clearly what our Father is like. We are enabled to discern and discover what God's intentions are for us. The light of His presence, His person, expressed in His Word by His Spirit, does disclose to us what His desires are for us. We can see the direction in which He is taking us. We can find out what our destination will be. We can walk with Him in happy harmony surrounded by light, hour by hour.

The Parallel of Parenthood

Here I would like to again resort to the parallel of parenthood in order for you to fully grasp the concept of what is meant by harmony between our Father and us.

A newborn child has rather restricted vision at first. Its eyes do not always focus sharply. Things may appear to be a bit blurred. Its father's face and mother's smile may be only dimly perceived. But as the weeks move along, the eyes of the youngster strengthen, sharpen, gradually bringing objects all around it into distinct detail.

These are the days when with fluttering heart and anxious watchfulness the parents expectantly wait for the first fleeting smiles of recognition from their offspring. They yearn and long to see the youngster gurgle and coo with contentment when they come into view. They will spend hours encouraging the child to look at them, recognize them, then break into a broad, happy smile of recognition.

As the youngster grows, the great bond between him and his parent is to be able to see him. The child wants to be in the same room. He wants to be in close company. He wants to know what the parent is doing. He wants to go where he goes, he endeavors to do what the adult does. He follows in his footsteps, tagging and toddling along behind like a veritable shadow.

As life goes on, the youngster constantly keeps the parent in view, provided of course the parent is at home to be within sight. It is the child's paramount concern to copy, emulate, learn, and mature from this intimate, ongoing companionship. Both consciously and subconsciously it is becoming like its mentor. Often by the time it is a teenager it will have taken on many of the special character qualities and habits of conduct which it acquired from the parent.

Ultimately it may even be said of the young person, "Why, you are the spitting image of your Dad!"

The extent to which this can happen is well illustrated by an incident in Africa that thrilled me many years ago.

I left my home in Kenya at the age of eighteen to take university training overseas. Fourteen long years passed by before I was able to return and visit my boyhood haunts again. In the meantime my parents had both passed away. So when I went back I did so without any special welcome or fanfare.

What I wanted more than anything else was simply to stroll quietly again in some of the spots where Dad and I had so often walked in company together. We had often hiked together, hunted together, and visited the native villages together.

One of these belonged to the local chief. Coming unannounced, quietly, I walked through the circle of huts where his retinue of some seventeen assorted wives each had their home.

Two women sat in the warm morning sun shelling corn

and talking happily. As I passed by, one of them suddenly exclaimed to the other: "See that man! He walks exactly like Bwana Keller used to walk!"

Gently I turned around and went over to them. In their own dialect, which I had learned as a lad, I said softly, "I am his son!"

In utter amazement both women leaped to their feet. Flinging their hands over their wide-open mouths in typical African astonishment, they were momentarily speechless. Then suddenly both burst out: "Bwana Keller must have risen from the dead. He must be alive. You walk like him. You talk like him. You look like him. You must be him!"

It was a moving moment in my life. God used it to drive home a powerful parallel. Can the same be said of me and my Heavenly Father? Is the imprint, the mark of His character on me this way? Have we kept such close company? Can it be seen that I walk with Him?

The Role and Nature of Conscience

The answer to that question lies in the realm of whether or not I walk with God in a clear, unclouded conscience. It lies in whether or not I see Him as He really is. It lies in knowing, understanding, and complying with His will and wishes for me in a pure conscience.

Let me explain. Conscience is not the voice of God. Conscience is not a contrivance designed by deity to make the wandering wayfarer uncomfortable. Conscience is not some trick used by God to prick and prod us into proper behavior, as so many people wrongly suppose.

Conscience is a generous, gracious gift from God to man's spirit. Conscience is the God-given capacity of my spirit to comprehend the loftiest, noblest, purest prospect presented to it. Conscience is the faculty of a man's spirit to see, hold in view, and reach toward the highest standard shown to it.

Put in very plain language we can say that conscience is the eyesight of the spirit. With it a person perceives and holds in view whatever may be shown to the spirit as being either of God's character or God's intentions.

Depending upon whatever is presented to it, a person's conscience will determine not only what he believes but also what he does.

For example, the Hindu widow's conscience convinces her that she should fling herself on the funeral pyre of her deceased husband. She has been brought to "see" this as the most noble act she can perform to appease her gods.

A pagan African woman will, if she gives birth to twin girls, bury both alive. Her conscience is convinced that this is proper. Her pagan conscience constrains her to commit this act because it is the finest, most self-sacrificing step she can take.

A Muslim, in good conscience, without any compunction will slay an infidel. It is his guarantee of glory. He has done the will of Allah. He has acted with a clear Muslim conscience.

Paul, formerly the petulant, self-righteous Pharisee, persecuted the early Christians with intense hatred. In all good conscience he hounded and harried them all across the country from city to city, sure he was doing God's will. Then he "saw" the bright light on the Damascus road and was given a new conscience.

From all the foregoing it may be seen that a "Hindu conscience," a "pagan conscience," a "Muslim conscience," and a "Pharisaical conscience" simply are not the voice of God.

Rather, conscience is the way a spirit "sees" or perceives God to be, and what it understands and holds in view as God's will and wishes.

Conscience for the Christian

In the Word of God, three words are always used to describe a healthy conscience. It is called either "good" or "pure" or "clear," depending on the translation.

In contradistinction it is also referred to as "evil" or "seared" when not functioning properly. Sometimes the word *dead* is also used.

Put another way we might say that our spiritual eyesight is either clear or blurred. It is either excellent or impaired. It is wholesome and healthy or it is damaged and blinded.

And how we see God and His will determines very largely how we live and walk with Him.

The interesting and surprising thing about conscience is that it is almost always discussed in God's Word together with faith. Our faith is dependent upon and determined by the condition of our conscience (1 Timothy 1:5–19; Hebrews 9:12–15; 10:16–22).

Faith is my positive response to God Himself and to His Word to the point where I will act in confidence. The more clearly I see Him, the more intimately I perceive His will with a clear conscience, the more readily I respond in rugged, fearless faith. If my conscience is clouded, my sight of Him is impaired. Then my faith falters and I cannot walk with Him in happy light.

> *Conscience is to my spirit,*
> *What sight is to my body, and mind is*
> *To my soul.*

Conscience functions in the spirit just as eyesight does for the body or mind does for the soul.

The growing child sees its father's face; watches his movements; observes his behavior and habits with exciting interest. Light falling on the father is reflected back to the youngster's eyes. The child sees. The child learns to know, to love, to follow the father because his eyes watch every move the parent makes.

Our Heavenly Father, in His own wondrous way, reveals Himself to us. The light of His own truth; the illumination of His own person; the self-revelation of what He is like and how He acts is made acutely clear to us in Christ.

> That which was from the beginning,
> Which we have heard,
> Which we have seen with our eyes,
> Which we have looked upon,
> And our hands have handled,
> Of the Word of life;
>
> (For the life was manifested,
> And we have seen it, and bear witness,
> And shew unto you that eternal life,
> Which was with the Father,
> And was manifested unto us;)
>
> That which we have seen and heard
> Declare we unto you,
> That ye also may have fellowship with us:
> And truly our fellowship is with the Father,
> And with his Son Jesus Christ.
>
> And these things write we unto you,
> That your joy may be full.

This then is the message which
We have heard of him,
And declare unto you,
That God is light,
And in him is no darkness at all.

1 John 1:1–5

If we want to walk with Him, talk with Him, move along through life with Him, then indeed our conscience must be focused on Him. Then faith functions fearlessly because it sees Him clearly, comprehends what He is doing, and quietly invests full confidence in His trustworthy character.

Just as a growing child comes to see clearly with its physical eyes, so it also comes to "see" increasingly with its mind. We call this process learning, understanding, comprehending. When a new idea, concept, or noble aspiration is presented to it, it responds by saying, "I see, I understand, I get it." If lofty ideals, great truths, and worthwhile objectives are set before the child, it can lay hold of them, hold them in view, and attain great stature in life.

Exactly the same process takes place with the conscience of God's child. In His generosity and magnanimous goodwill God has shown us clearly what are His ideals, standards, aims, and aspirations for us. If our conscience is good we will hold these clearly in view. We will see precisely what His will is for us. We will aspire to and attain His best purposes for us as we walk with Him in openness.

Unfortunately This Does Not Always Happen— Things Can Go Wrong

With conscience, just as with our eyes or in our minds, vision can be impaired. Eyesight can be damaged or distorted. One can become blinded.

It only takes a tiny gnat; a bit of dust; a small cinder from a fire; a puff of smoke to dim our vision. Our eyes pain. They stream tears. We cannot see. Our sight is gone. Everything becomes blurred and black and badly distorted.

Sometimes the difficulty is less sudden or dramatic but even more dangerous. Cataracts or glaucoma gradually cast a cloud across the vision. Eyesight becomes seared and strained. Eventually we may be totally blind.

Exactly the same thing can happen to conscience, and unless prompt and immediate steps are taken to correct the trouble we can no longer walk in light, but grope about in darkness.

In the realm of our minds, too, things can go very wrong. Indulgence in excess alcohol, drugs, and perverted pastimes; exposure to false philosophies or ideas will impair and distort our minds. We cannot comprehend clearly. We become deranged. We may even totally "blow our minds." No longer can we see, recognize, or respond to those values which are fine, true, beautiful, and worthwhile (Philippians 4:4–8).

Our view of God, in Christ, our comprehension in spirit of precisely what His wishes are for us, can likewise become obscured and distorted by a conscience that is damaged and corrupted. The net result is that we find we cannot respond in faith to Him or His Word.

God becomes distant. Christ at best is seen only dimly. His Word appears to us distorted, unreal, unreliable. We find we do not want to respond to light from it. Instead we recoil from its illumination. We prefer the darkness. Our conscience hurts. It, too, cries out and streams tears. It pains. But we have no inclination to walk with God. We do not want to walk in the light. Even praying becomes a problem. Darkness descends.

How Conscience Is Corrupted

There are basically three main causes for a corrupted (evil) conscience. Each of them impairs our spiritual sight so that we can no longer walk joyfully with God Our Father, or with our fellowman.

1) The sins of simple disobedience.

Like little gnats; specks of dust, burning sparks, flying fragments of steel, broken glass, or sawdust that enters the eye, acts of deliberate disobedience immediately produce enormous problems.

When foreign matter enters our eyes we drop whatever we are doing, we struggle to extricate the offending fly or speck of sawdust.

Until it is removed and the eye is cleared, we cannot see either for ourselves or to help another. *Light is shut out!*

This is why Jesus told the simple story of the man who got a speck of sawdust in his eyes. He could not see for himself, let alone derive help from the fellow with a larger splinter in his vision. He had no light to see, so how could he help another in darkness?

The instant a person, with eyes wide open, does what he or she knows to be wrong, they have allowed foreign matter to fly into their line of vision. Spiritual sight is impaired. Conscience is seared. It cries out for cleansing. And until the offending object (sin) is removed, vision is distorted. One simply stumbles and staggers about in darkness befuddled and bewildered.

This explains why Christians who have sin in their lives often seek for light and illumination for their next step, but none comes. It is not that God refuses to give light on the path. He does not withhold illumination. The difficulty lies in the conscience of the Christians. The sight is blinded by sin, and so they shut their sight to the light of the truth. They simply cannot see to take the next step. They cannot walk in the light.

> If we say that we have fellowship with him, and walk in darkness, we lie, and do not the truth
>
> 1 John 1:6

This explains why one with sin in his life cannot lead another to meet the Master.

At every step where we disobey we leave our conscience wide open and vulnerable to the intrusion of sin that blinds us to God and His will. Prompt and immediate measures must be taken to clear the conscience. Sight simply must be restored. To fail to do this is to blunder about blindly in darkness. We will see how shortly.

2) *Soulish sensuality.*

The second chief cause for a beclouded conscience is self-indulgence in the realm of our souls. We allow our minds, emotions, and wills to dominate and override our spiritual intuition and conscience and communion with Christ.

Like a cloud of dust or smoke that sweeps over and

around us we become engulfed in sensuality. We say to our-selves, "After all, I am only human. I'm only doing what is natural. There can't be anything wrong with it, everybody does it." And so we are caught up in a whole sinister smoke screen of excuses for our selfish, self-centered behavior.

The upshot is that conscience is clouded. It cries out for relief from the enfolding darkness. It wants to escape the fog of false ideas, worldly philosophies, and perverted pleasures. But all too often we stubbornly refuse to remove ourselves from the danger. We adamantly defend our decision to "do our own thing" despite the consequence of searing our con-science. The result is that we cannot see God or His wishes for us.

Instead we will often indulge in other feverish activity or work that we feel compensates for our otherwise selfish pur-suits. For example, a man who makes business his absolute priority in life will try to appease his conscience by saying, "Then I have more money for the Lord's work." This is sheer flimflam. It is self-deception. God's Word calls the whole show *dead works*. And it says our conscience simply has to be cleared of all such clutter that beclouds our walk with God (Hebrews 9:14).

Spiritual truth cannot be clouded over. It cannot be fogged up with our feelings. It must be kept ever in clear view. Our Father God must be first and foremost in our vi-sion. His character, His conduct, His conversation must be the center of our focus as we walk with Him.

3) *The subtle insinuations of Satan.*

Just as cataracts or glaucoma gradually, insidiously creep across the eyes to slowly blind them, so the subtle suggestions of the enemy can creep into our conscience. We can end up with what the Scriptures call an evil conscience (bad vision).

It is Satan who suggests to us so often that God really is not reliable. He tells us that Christ is not trustworthy. He insinuates that the things of the Spirit are just a bunch of old-fashioned superstitions. He casts a cloud of doubt over God's Word. He questions its veracity and validity. He implants conflicting questions in the church. He befogs issues with doctrinal differences. He produces division and discord amongst God's people. Satan is the god of this world. He does everything in his power to blind the minds and corrupt the consciences of those who believe. He does not want the glorious good news and bright light of Christ's presence and person to penetrate the darkness of his realm. He dreads to have us see God in all His lovely splendor, justice, and goodness.

> But if our gospel be hid, it is hid to them that are lost: In whom the god of this world hath blinded the minds of them which believe not, lest the light of the glorious gospel of Christ, who is the image of God, should shine unto them.
>
> 2 Corinthians 4:3, 4

Unfortunately many fall for his falsehoods. They become blinded. They cannot see God. They are not conscious of Christ. They are not sensitive to God's gracious Spirit. They go on groping in darkness, deceived and deluded. Often they do the most atrocious things, claiming to be doing God's will. They call evil good and good evil.

One cannot walk with God that way. It spells utter disaster!

The Cure for a Corrupt Conscience

There are three simple, effective steps one can take to keep a clear conscience.

1) First, get it cleansed!

The instant it begins to burn, to cry, to stream tears, remove the offending object. Get it out into the open.

The speck, the fly, the splinter, the grit must come out of the eye. In our home we carry a constant supply of camomile tea. When brewed, then used to wash the eyes, it removes foreign matter and brings instant relief and healing. Sight is quickly restored.

The grand old Apostle John urges us in these words:

But if we walk in the light, as he is in the light, we have fellowship one with another, and the blood of Jesus Christ his Son cleanseth us from all sin.

If we say that we have no sin, we deceive ourselves, and the truth is not in us. If we confess our sins, he is faithful and just to forgive us our sins, and to cleanse us from all unrighteousness.

1 John 1:7-9

Come quickly to Christ. Let Him cleanse you. Confess your wrongdoings. Apologize. Make things right with Him, with others. Allow the cleansing power of His forgiveness, flowing to you because of His blood shed on your behalf, to sweep away the offending sins that make your conscience corrupt.

Let Him restore your spiritual sight. Let His hands touch your eyes to see Himself. Let His Spirit apply the healing ointment of His own presence to your burning, sin-seared spirit.

2) *Repent in genuine remorse.*

If I am standing by a campfire or at the side of a country road, and suddenly a gust of wind engulfs me in a cloud of smoke or billowing dust, I do something about it. Before I am blinded, I get out of there in a hurry. I quit the place at once.

That is what repentance means. It means turning my back to the danger that threatens me. It means I hate it, so I remove myself at once from that situation. To repent is to quit. I don't hang around the smoke and dust hoping it will go away. I get out fast. I'm done with it.

If we are to walk with God in honesty, strength, and goodwill we simply have to be done with the old soulish self-life of sin and sensuality and subversion. Get out and get moving with God.

3) *Obey God simply, immediately, sincerely.*

No more excuses. No more flimflam. No more pussy-footing with false ideas and worldly ideologies. Just do what

God in Christ asks you to do. Respond in positive faith to what you see clearly in His Word you should do. Step out to act on what His Spirit shows you is appropriate. He will honor your faith. You will walk with Him in a clear conscience, a powerful person, going places with God—*walking by faith, not by feelings.*

3

Walking With God in Spirit of Communion

What Communion With God Means

When two people are in harmony with one another they are said to be in communion. There is a oneness between them. There is open, unclouded interaction. This sort of clear communication brings enormous pleasure and benefit to both parties. It generates goodwill, develops deep, abiding friendship, and fosters powerful faith between the two people.

It can be exactly the same with us and God. In fact, a part of the original motivation that moved God to create man in the beginning was His desire to have sons and daughters with whom He could commune in spirit. We are told this very clearly in Ephesians chapter one:

For consider what he has done—before the foundation of the world he chose us to be, in Christ, his children, holy and blameless in his sight. He planned, in his love, that we should be adopted as his own children through Jesus Christ—this was his will and pleasure that we

might praise that glorious generosity of his which he
granted to us in his Beloved.

Ephesians 1:4–6 PHILLIPS

This is a sublime picture portrayed for us under the inspiration of God's own gracious Spirit. We see ourselves
brought into the family of our Heavenly Father. We see our
complete acceptance as His children because of the great
generosity He shows toward us. We see God yearning and
longing for us to learn to commune with Him at the intimate
and profound level of child with parent. Hand in hand we
walk with God our Father.

This is communion in the spirit. It is constant and continuous communication prompted by profound pleasure in
each other's company. It is not some religious rote or ritual.
It is two spirits who enjoy each other, who revel in each
other's company.

The Means of Communion

Over and over throughout my various devotional books
the fact has been emphasized that God our Father is not out
somewhere distant in the immensity of space. To be sure, He
does occupy all the universe. He reveals that to us over and
over by His own Word. But for us as His children, He is
here. He is at hand. He is, as Paul put it to the Athenians,
not far from any one of us. In truth it is in Him that we move
and live and have our being. We are in fact His offspring
whom He holds with His hand. (*Read* Acts 17:24–31.)

This being the case, it follows that He has made proper
provision for us to walk with Him, to talk with Him, to share

with Him, to commune with Him personally, privately, profoundly.

There are, basically, seven ways whereby God and man commune in spirit. Four of these come from Him to us. Three, in turn, come from us to Him; God and man walking hand in hand.

It is important that we put much more emphasis on what Christ has to communicate to us than on what we might have to say to Him. There is far too much preoccupation in Christian circles today with man's predicaments rather than with God's proclamations. If all of us would concentrate and focus on what God says to us, we would soon become powerful people. Christ is constantly endeavoring to commune with us through His Word. Let us be sensitive, open, receptive to His Spirit who reveals God in these ways.

1. God communes with me through His Word spoken—*the Scriptures.*
2. God communes with me through Jesus Christ. He was the Word made Man: God in human form.
3. God communes with me through His Spirit of Truth, who leads and teaches me from His Word, who speaks to me in His own still, small voice of inner conviction by His Word.
4. God communes with me through those people in whom He resides; through the providential events of life He arranges; through the natural world of His own wondrous creation.

In turn God has provided three ways whereby we can commune with Him, or, if you will, reach out to touch Him.

1. Man communes with God through prayer.
2. Man communes with God through praise, gratitude, and adoration.
3. Man communes with God through profound stillness, his spirit quiet, contemplative, worshipful, open, available, receptive.

Entire books, lofty discussions, endless debates, multitudes of sermons, and enormous study have been given to each of these seven means of communion. It would seem nothing new can be added here. Nonetheless I wish to examine each in a very practical way. Each will be reduced to its simplest form so that the reader can apply it to his/her walk with God.

But before doing this there are several profound principles which underlie any effort we may make to commune with God in spirit. The first is that we must come to really know Him. Or if we don't, at least we must desire to do so. It is pointless to presume that we can commune with someone who is not known or whom we do not care to know.

Communion is a two-way intercourse, the touching of two lives. It is a two-way interaction. It is a two-way correspondence. Please do not play games with God. He can be known. Communion in spirit is possible.

Second, we must commune with Him in good conscience. What He discloses and declares to us we must hold clearly in view. He simply refuses to reveal either Himself or His will and intentions to those who in turn refuse to respond, who prefer to remain in darkness. God, by virtue of His very nature, is repelled by the pride, arrogance, and self-assurance of self-centered, selfish spirits. He sets Himself against them (James 4:1–10). So walk with Him humbly in light.

Third, as with a good conscience, and in clear spiritual sight we walk softly with Him, we will find enormous faith in Him. We will respond positively in purposeful action to comply with His wishes. This is to walk with Him in quiet confidence, in open light. It is to sense and discover a deep, compelling communion between Him and us.

1) *God communes with me through His Word.*

Our Lord Himself, when He was here amongst us as a man, made the stunning, stabbing statement, *"It is the spirit that quickeneth; the flesh profiteth nothing: the words that I speak unto you, they are spirit, and they are life"* (John 6:63).

God, very God, articulates Himself in language we can understand. He does communicate His will and wishes to us. He does reveal His character to us. He does disclose His conduct. He throws the illuminating light of His truth on the path we are to take in life.

This is why the Scriptures must be taken seriously. They must be studied. They must be read and reread. They are His love letters to us. They should elicit a profound, compelling response from us. (*Read all of Psalm 119 prayerfully.*)

It takes time, a lot of time, precious time, to listen, to hear, to understand, "to see" what He is saying. Most of us are slow of spirit, preoccupied with our petty pursuits and petty pride. We are not sensitive to His Spirit speaking to us in His Word. Too often we are preoccupied with the workaday world and whirl of pleasure around us.

If you want to hear from God, if you want Christ to commune with you, here are some simple steps you can take in your walk with Him.

Get alone in some quiet, private spot with His Word. Before opening it, ask Him sincerely to speak through it. Read slowly, deliberately, steadily through each book of it. Concentrate intently on what you read. *Let God show you Himself and His will!*

In a private journal, with the date, write down clearly in your own words what He said to you for the day.

Thank Him for being honest and faithful to you.

Go out to walk with Him through that day, *doing whatever He showed you to do.*

Recall throughout the day what it was He revealed to you. If there is opportunity, share this insight with another person.

The Word of God will become to you more than a Bible. It will be His Spirit transmitting *truth to your spirit.*

2) *God communes with me through Jesus Christ.*

There is no person in all the world, nor in the entire history of the human race, about whom more has been written than Jesus Christ. I, myself, have given many, many years of study, meditation, and prayer to His person, recording what I could in the book *Rabboni.* It is the most important work of my life.

No one can do anything better with his time than give special attention to Jesus Christ. He is not just another historical figure who set foot briefly on the stage of human history. He is not just another religious teacher who founded another world religion. He is not just another deity amongst many strange gods devised by man's imagination. He is not just a divine, superb idea expressing supernatural doctrine.

Jesus Christ is God, very God. He always is! He existed

before planet earth was ever formed for human habitation. He brought it into being. He is present all through its agonizing ongoing. He breaks through from the supernatural realm to be born amongst us as a man—*God incognito—God in mufti—God in human guise.*

He lives amongst us; works amongst us; ministers amongst us; teaches truth amongst us; suffers amongst us; dies in our stead amongst us; rises amongst us; ascends back to His former splendor amongst us; He is alive amongst us!

He is God, very God, revealing God to us. He is, as Paul put it, "... the visible expression of the invisible God ..." (Colossians 1:15 PHILLIPS).

Jesus Christ communicates to us the very character of God. He conveys to us the conduct of God. He assures our questing spirits that through Himself, God very God speaks to us, touches us, in unmistakable terms.

If you wish to walk with God, then walk with the Living Lord. Spend time with your Saviour. Befriend your Friend. Talk to Him. Think about Him. Let the wondrous impact of His Person impress itself upon your spirit. Keep company with Christ, allow Him to become your constant companion on the road of life you travel together. He is alive. He is here, now, today. Turn to Him.

3) *God communes with me through His Spirit.*

During the past thirty years a large segment of Christendom has suddenly awakened to the presence of the Person of God the Holy Spirit. This acute awareness has enlivened many who formerly were enmeshed in rigid ritual or formal orthodoxy. Unfortunately, too, there has come with this renewal some spurious teaching and counterfeit experiences which have misled some who truly longed to walk with God in truth.

God's Spirit is the Spirit of Truth. He is the great Illuminator. He does not draw attention to Himself. He focuses our affection on Christ and on our Father.

Howbeit when he, the Spirit of truth, is come, he will guide you into all truth: for he shall not speak of himself; but whatsoever he shall hear, that shall he speak: and he will shew you things to come.

He shall glorify me: for he shall receive of mine, and shall shew it unto you.

All things that the Father hath are mine: therefore said I, that he shall take of mine, and shall shew it unto you.
John 16:13–15

He, the Spirit of God, is just that! He is the One who transmits to me not only truth about God but actually conveys to me the very life of the risen, living Christ as well. He is the One who is my constant Companion. He is my Counselor. He is my Comrade-in-Arms on the trail of life we tramp together. He is the One who says to me in the depths of my spirit, "This is the way, walk in it." (Read John 14, 15, 16, and 17 prayerfully.)

It is the Spirit of God who will enter your spirit and share life with you, touch you, inspire you, enliven you, as you make yourself available to His own purposes for you. This is not meant to be passive and phlegmatic, open to subversive, counterfeit spirits (evil) which proliferate on every side. Rather it is to be alert, awake, available, eager to act in prompt obedience to His inner urging—*His own presence. He is God resident within.*

He speaks to us, touches us, teaches us truth through God's own Word, which He Himself inspired. He lays upon our spirits a profound inner conviction that "I ought, or I ought not," in our walk with Him. He gives Himself to us in generous measure (Acts 5:32). He transforms and leads us in the path of right living.

4) *God communes with me through the people in whom He resides; through providential events; through His natural created universe.*

These three means of communication are so obvious that they require very little elaboration here.

Almost all of us have had men or women cross our paths who were obviously deeply and significantly walking with God. Without pretense or ostentation they made an enormous impact upon us. Through their character and conduct we got a new glimpse of God. We knew they had been with Jesus. They walked in company with God's gracious Spirit.

Just knowing them induced within our spirits an intense, inner desire to know and walk with God in the same way. Some of them God used to touch our lives and commune with us in tangible terms.

Then there are the circumstantial events of our everyday, common, human experiences whereby our Father constantly alerts us to His presence. His compassionate arrangement of our affairs with our best interests in mind stills our spirits and moves us to turn to Him in enormous gratitude.

Looking back over the trails we have trod together, whether it be for the last twenty-four hours or past twenty-four years, there comes that acute, stabbing, sweet awareness, "Oh, my Father, Your hand has been on me every step of the way. It has been You who has picked out the path. It is You who has kept my feet from falling. It is You who has been faithful as a Father to this wandering, wayward, sometimes willful child."

Learn to look for His hand in all the events of your life. Learn to thank Him for every incident. Adulate Him with your appreciation.

Finally there is the grandeur, the glory, the gentleness of our God shown to us in the created universe all around us. In stars and streams; in mountains and meadows; in grass and trees; in oceans and plains; He conveys strength, inspiration, and uplift to our seeking spirits.

> The heavens declare the glory of God; and the firmament sheweth his handywork. Day unto day uttereth speech, and night unto night sheweth knowledge. There is no speech nor language, where their voice is not heard. Their line is gone out through all the earth, and their words to the end of the world. In them hath he set a tabernacle for the sun.
>
> Psalms 19:1–4

I have written entire books on this theme, such as *Ocean Glory, Mountain Splendor,* and *Still Waters.* I need say no more.

Get outdoors and discover, "Oh, God, You are here!
Walk with me!"

5) *Man communes with God in prayer.*

We turn now, very briefly, to discuss how we commune
with God in Christ, by His Spirit, from man's side.

We must see that even here the initiative really begins
with God. His own winsome Spirit touching, quickening,
enlivening mine makes me want to commune with Him. He
does this and actually expresses it often in terms which can
find no articulation in human language (Romans 8:25–27).

The most profound prayer any person ever engages in
seldom finds expression in human syllables. It is the stirring
of our spirits by God's Spirit in such a way that we long with
enormous inner longing. We are still, silent, subdued,
yearning, knowing, seeing Him whom to know is life eternal.

Our Lord made it abundantly clear that much of our
praying, done either in public or in private, was really
pagan. (Read Matthew 6:5–15.) The repetitive, thoughtless,
mouthing of tired old phrases, or ritualistic rhetoric, is not
the manner in which a man consciously communes with his
Creator. My book *A Layman Looks at the Lord's Prayer* can
help some in this area.

It is God's Spirit who impresses upon our spirits what we
are to pray about. Seeing clearly what His concerns are, we
proceed in faith to respond by placing these petitions before
Him. This is the prayer of faith. He then honors and answers
those prayers in the profound way which is most appropriate both to His will and our needs.

This is what is meant by Christ being both the Author and

the Finisher of our faith. Our prayers are conceived in our spirits by Him. They are consummated in His own good time in His own best way. And for all of this we give Him our genuine gratitude.

Communing with Christ this way, we come to walk with God in quiet strength, serene stability, and constant assurance.

"Oh, Lord, it is wonderful to know You, talk to You, and trust You."

6) *Man communes with God in praise.*

As we walk with God, learning to recognize His hand upon us through His Word; through His Son; through His Spirit; through other people; through His arrangement of our affairs; through the beauty of His earth; through the impact of prayer answered; there will spring up from within our spirits an overflowing fountain of praise, appreciation, and gratitude.

This is absolutely inevitable. It does in fact become the central, compelling motivation for a person's desire to please God; to walk with Him in harmony; to enjoy His presence; to love Him because He has first loved us; to literally live for Him.

Praise of this sort embraces the whole of my life. It is not the mere articulation of pretty phrases or pious-sounding platitudes. Genuine praise is an entire life lived in humble gratitude and wholesome appreciation for who God is and what He has done. It is a clean-cut, shining, simple walk with the most wondrous Friend in all the world.

This is what is meant by God inhabiting the praise of His people. He actually deigns, in magnanimous generosity, to come and reside with such a person. He lives with him, talks with him, shares life with him, loves him, enjoys walking with him.

> Jesus answered and said unto him, If a man love me, he will keep my words: and my Father will love him, and we will come unto him, and make our abode with him.
>
> John 14:23

A true life of praise to God implies three salient things:

1) I acknowledge He is God, very God, and that He arranges all my affairs with only my best interests in mind because He loves me. This applies even when things appear to my view to be awry.

2) I accept everything that happens along life's path as His provision. This is the path of peace. I do not fight life, trying to change everything or everyone. They, instead, are accepted and allowed to modify and mature me.

3) I approve of what God has done and how He does it. This sets His Spirit free to do abundantly more than I can ever hope or imagine. I praise Him that it is He who is at work in me both to will and to do of His good pleasure (Ephesians 3:16–21; Philippians 2:12–15). This is to walk with God in peace, power, and praise.

7) *Man communes with God in quietness.*

We live in a busy, bustling world. Our society is the product of a clamorous culture. Life is noisy. It is often rude, increasingly crude. Enormous pressures of a hundred sorts exert a profound impact upon us. The tensions of our technology have been transmitted to our life-style. We are, for the most part, people driven by enormous desires; aroused by insatiable appetites; tantalized by tempting tastes; inflamed by passing pursuits and passions.

So we rush to and fro. We are people on the go. And amid all the mayhem God calls to us softly, persistently, patiently, and says: "Be still, and know that I am God . . ." (Psalms 46:10).

Too many of us never seem to believe this. We are too busy; too preoccupied with the pressures upon us; too hounded and harried to call a halt and get alone with God.

In spite of this, may I urge you to do so, even if your family, friends, and other associates consider you odd, queer, and perhaps a bit "touched." Take time each day, even if only for a few fleeting moments, to get absolutely away from those around you. Get alone with God. Seek some secluded spot. Close the inner door to the inner room of your inner spirit. Be still. Be silent. Be serene.

In utter quietness open your spirit to the Spirit of God. Sigh the words that young Samuel spoke: ". . . Speak; for thy servant heareth" (1 Samuel 3:10).

There will be impressed by His Spirit, upon yours, that word; that inner conviction; that growing compulsion which can come to you only from God your Father. He will speak peace to your spirit. He will impart Himself to you. He will engulf you with His goodwill and His good cheer. He will assure you, *"I am with you always—even to the end of this noisy, high-pressure, restless age—walk with Me in quiet confidence!"*

SECTION
II
WALKING WITH GOD
IN MY SOUL

CHAPTER

1

Walking With God in My Mind

The Soul or Person of Man

As with his spirit, so likewise with his soul: Man has three main realms of activity. For purposes of simplicity these are referred to as *mind, emotions,* and *will.*

With the mind a person thinks, reasons, contemplates, learns, makes deductions, studies, plans, imagines, and re-members. It is in essence the capacity to think and learn, with the combined ability to apply whatever knowledge has been so acquired to new situations.

All of this is sometimes called our *thought-life.*

In this century the mind of man has been given enormous study. The social sciences of psychology and psychiatry are devoted to the mind. Quite literally hundreds of books have been written on the subject. Thousands and thousands of university and college students have made this their lifetime study and career.

Much of modern thought, modern society, and modern man has been shaped and molded by the contemporary world view of the mind. Unfortunately for many of God's people, this has led to enormous turmoil and tension.

The reason I say this is because some men and women who work in the fields of psychology and psychiatry behave as though, and believe sincerely, man is made up only of mind and body.

This concept is current in some Christian circles as well, so much so that Christians often seek the world's remedies for so-called sick minds. They turn to humanistic theories and scientific technology for treatment of this segment of their souls. They assume scientific methods grounded on thinking which does not take God into consideration at all can remedy their condition.

Unhappily, multitudes find neither comfort in the psychologist's counseling nor cure in the psychiatrist's couch.

The Mind Becomes a Battleground

With the increasing complexity of modern society, man's mind is being exposed to ever-increasing tension and turmoil. The input from the mass media, whether radio, television, literature, schooling, or social intercourse, puts enormous pressures upon our thought patterns. No longer is life a simple process of growing up gently amid a small circle of intimate family contacts. Today all the trouble, all the turmoil, all the tragedy, all the tensions of the entire planet are dropped on the doorstep of our minds every day.

It was never intended that we should become so deeply enmeshed in all the heartache and hardships of the entire human family, worldwide. Added to this horrendous burden is the chaos, the confusion of living our own private lives amid increasingly complex circumstances.

Amid the temptations, the tragedy, and the tension of our

twentieth century, many dear people wonder sincerely and ask earnestly if it is indeed possible to walk with God quietly and serenely in their thought-life.

Some seeking souls find their minds are a muddle. They have never been taught that Christ really does desire to control this area. They have never discovered that serenity comes only as they surrender to the supreme sovereignty of God's gracious Spirit.

Often their thoughts are a veritable battlefield, where the forces of good and evil contest the ground of their minds. Outwardly such people may put on a fine pretense of poise. Inwardly they may well be engulfed in violent struggles. Terrible thoughts, evil imaginations, cruel censure, formidable fantasies, and twisted thinking may surge through their souls.

If we are to understand why this happens, we do well to see what God says to us on the subject.

Who Manipulates Our Minds?

Most of us assume rather naively that we are masters of our own minds. We imagine that we are in charge of our mental processes. God's revelation to us is otherwise.

In the case of the non-Christian, the nonbeliever, the mind is impervious to and unenlightened by the truth of God's Word. In fact, it is incapable of seeing or laying hold of eternal verities.

But if our gospel [the Good News of God's redemption in Christ] be hid, it is hid to them that are lost: In whom the god of this world [Satan] hath blinded the minds of them which believe not, lest the light of the glorious gospel of Christ, who is the image of God, should shine unto them.

2 Corinthians 4:3, 4

This explains why the non-Christian is incapable of walking with God in harmony. He is in darkness. As Jesus said so often, "Eyes you have but you see not. Ears you have but you hear not" (*see* Mark 8:18).

The things of God appear as utter folly to unregenerate man. His mind has never been converted (changed), illuminated, or sensitized to the Spirit of God.

Then there are so-called carnal Christians. These are what I call "halfway" people. They have started to step out and follow Christ, but their thoughts are still conditioned and controlled by the culture of the world in which they live. Their old selfish nature and self-centered preoccupation color all of their thinking.

Paul, with devastating forthrightness, describes such people in his letter to the Romans:

> If men comply with their lower nature, their thoughts are shaped by the lower nature; if with their spiritual nature, by the spiritual. Thoughts shaped by the lower nature mean death; thoughts shaped by the spiritual mean life and peace. For thoughts shaped by the lower nature mean a state of enmity to God. They do not submit to God's law, and indeed cannot. Those who obey the lower nature cannot please God.

Romans 8:5–8 WEYMOUTH

From the foregoing it can be clearly seen that it is fatal to assume that one can walk with God, be in company with

Christ, and enjoy the leading of His Spirit while dominated by selfish self-interest. The two are mutually exclusive.

Christ's Claim Upon My Mind

It should be obvious to the reader that if there is to be harmony between me and God; if there is to be any sort of closeness with Christ; if there is to be any oneness with God's Spirit, we must be of one mind. It is the only way to walk with Him in openness and goodwill.

We simply cannot be at enmity with God in our thoughts. Yet many are, who at the same time claim to be walking with Him. This is pure self-delusion.

God appeals to us again and again throughout His Word to come to terms with Him.

For example: "Come now, and let us reason together, saith the Lord: though your sins be as scarlet, they shall be as white as snow; though they be red like crimson, they shall be as wool" (Isaiah 1:18).

He invites us to turn ourselves over to the impact of His own person upon us. He urges us to so expose ourselves to His presence that our thought processes will be transformed. He invites us to come to Him in order that His mind might become ours.

I beseech you therefore, brethren, by the mercies of God, that ye present your bodies a living sacrifice, holy, acceptable unto God, which is your reasonable service. And be not conformed to this world: but be ye transformed by the renewing of your mind, that ye may prove what is that good, and acceptable, and perfect, will of God.

Romans 12:1, 2

This transformation of which God's Word speaks is a total turnabout in our thinking. It means a very true and titanic turnaround. It is a complete conversion.

We speak so glibly about "saving souls." We bandy about the phrase "born again." We talk of being "converted to Christ." For most people these are just pious pap. But for the man or woman dead in earnest with God, who wants to know Him, walk with Him, and enjoy Him, it means, "My mind has to be changed. My thinking has to be altered. My thought-life has to be drastically altered."

In short, for a man's soul to be saved means his mind must come under Christ's control. There cannot be conflict.

How to Tell Who Controls My Mind

One need only ask himself a few searching questions to determine who manages his mind.

Do I hold worldly views and values?

Am I pompous, proud, petulant?

Do I center my thoughts on self-gratification?

Do I have wild, wicked, wretched thoughts welling up from within?

Do I indulge in disquieting daydreams, flagrant fantasies?

Do I entertain deceitful, scheming, insidious ideas?

Do I have serious doubts and misgivings about God?

For some the above are daily habits. Their minds are being perpetually polluted by perversion. They sense and know that they themselves are being prostituted by their inner thought processes. They at least recognize that such thoughts do not come from Christ.

Even the most untutored will realize that they are being subjected to strong stimuli and conditioning causes not of God. Here are some of the forces which exert control over our minds:

1) The conditioning of our own culture; worldly wisdom.
2) The impact of our family and friends, many of whom do not know Christ.
3) The emphasis of our educational system. For the most part it is without God and ignores Him completely.
4) The input of the media with its extreme devotion to pleasure, leisure, materialism, sex, and sensuality.
5) The false philosophies of modern thinkers; humanistic thinking.
6) Our blind devotion to science, with its reliance only on observable phenomena.
7) The proliferation of counterfeit religions; the upsurge of the occult; the whole spectrum of false cults.
8) The worldwide revolt against authority and law and order; the propensity to violence.

Amid all these perverse influences which play upon us, manipulating our minds and emotions, there is one perhaps more deceptive than all the rest. It is false teaching within the church itself. It is the increasing emphasis placed upon sensual experiences and stimulating, highly charged personal group encounters.

Innocent, ignorant, ill-taught people are urged to seek ecstatic experiences. They are exhorted to allow their minds to become passive. Unwittingly they are led to think they can hear special voices; see special visions; dream exotic dreams; receive unique revelations; indulge in diabolical diversions.

They are convinced that this is to be superspiritual. Somehow they think they have the mind of Christ. Little do they know their perilous, spiritual pride and awful religious arrogance come from counterfeit forces set against God. And to walk in that way is not to walk with Him. It is to follow the old sensual way of the world which has infiltrated the church. (Read 2 Timothy chapter 3 to chapter 4:8.)

In contradiction to all these false teachings, false ideologies, false life-styles which proliferate all around us, God's Word gives us some very clear and simple guidelines for our thinking.

1) We are told to turn away from the world's ways of thinking and behaving (2 Timothy 3:5).

2) We are told that when God enters our lives by His Spirit, He gives us a sound, disciplined mind: "For God hath not given us the spirit of fear; but of power, and of love [selflessness], and of a sound [disciplined] mind" (2 Timothy 1:7).

3) We are exhorted and instructed to allow the very mind, the attitudes, the thought processes of Christ to be ours (Philippians 2:11).

4) We are told emphatically to think on those things which are noble, true, and worthwhile (Philippians 4:1–9).

Cultivating the Mind of Christ

Solomon, the ancient sage granted enormous wisdom from God, made the profound statement that as a person thinks, so is he/she (Proverbs 23:7). Please note that he did not say they are what they think they are. Too many fall into the self-delusion of thinking they are something other than they really are. God's view strips away all self-deception.

This being the case, we must then take serious steps to come into agreement with God as to what He thinks about us. Only in this way can we walk together in quiet accord. Here are some helpful hints to cultivating the mind of Christ.

1) *Search your own soul.*

If we are serious about having harmony with God in the realm of our thought-life we do have to take a hard look at what occupies our minds the most. By saying this I am not advocating morbid introspection. Nor am I in any way suggesting we should wallow about in the muddy waters of our past.

But from time to time we must allow the illumination of the light of God's Word to flood the inner sanctuary of our souls. We must allow our private thought-life to be carefully scrutinized by God's holy, pure Spirit. What He there reveals to us as offensive to Him, contrary to God's will, and in conflict with the mind of Christ, must be swept away.

There must be an inner purging, definite purification. It is perfectly possible to have our thoughts and mind-set altered. God, by His Spirit, through His Word, wants to do this for us. *But we must want it as well.* Nothing in our thinking habits will ever alter unless we wish a change.

We must view sin seriously. We must see that all selfishness expressed in hostility, bitterness, criticism, jealousy, hatred, ill will, discontent, complaining, faultfinding, cruelty,

indifference, and deception are diametrically opposite to the
mind of Christ. Our sins grieve God deeply. To continue to
express and hold such inner attitudes creates enormous
strain and tension between us and Him.

2) *Real repentance.*

The entire subject of genuine repentance is not often
mentioned amongst some Christians. Yet it is one of the essential ongoing steps anyone must take who wishes to enter
upon a new walk with Christ in close communion.

Having been shown what is amiss in our inner attitudes
and habitual thought patterns, we must come to hate them
as God does. We must see them as repulsive as He does. We
must want to jettison and abandon them (Psalms 119).

To repent of wrong thinking and evil thoughts is to not
only despise and abhor our selfishness expressed in sinister
inner attitudes but also to turn away from them—*to quit
them.*

In order for this to take place we must turn to the Lord in
genuine earnestness. With intense longing to be remade, re-
vitalized, redirected, we implore Him to turn us around. We
ask Him to alter our inner attitudes. We invite Him to in-
vade us with His presence in the areas emptied of evil
thoughts (Jeremiah 31:18, 19).

3) *Being transformed by the renewal of our minds.*

If in truth our desires and requests to be remade are genuine, honest, and sincere, God will begin to change us. Our
alteration may be sudden, dramatic, and drastic or it may be
a gradual growth in godliness.

The expulsive impact of the presence of Christ at the center of our attention and our affections will dismiss the former self-centered preoccupation with *me* and *mine* and *I*. His interests will become ours. His aspirations and ambitions will assert themselves in our thinking. His values, standards, and priorities will steadily replace those worldly concepts which previously monopolized our minds.

In short we will surely, steadily acquire a new mind-set. As Paul put it so precisely in Colossians 3:2:

> Give your minds to the things that are above, not to the things that are on the earth. For you have died, and your life is hidden with Christ in God.
>
> WEYMOUTH

4) *The cross of Christ must be applied to my mind.*

Much confusion is found in Christian circles about the whole concept of the cross in our walk with God. It is not just a case of carrying a burden, putting up with difficult people, or even patiently enduring hardship.

The "cross" is the straightforward principle of a person dying to his sensual, selfish, self-centered interests and attitudes. It is the very simple ongoing process of daily (even hourly) saying no to wrong thoughts, evil thinking, rotten attitudes, and by the same standard, saying yes to the outlook and aspirations of God's Spirit who resides within us.

The cross cuts diametrically across the wrong views of the world; the false value systems of society; the perverseness, pride, and pollution of our own personalities; the preoccupation with transient possessions, power, and prestige; the

obsession with vanity, sensuality, and folly that character-
izes fallen humanity.

The cross means unlearning most of what we learned to
love in life.

5) *Being set free from wrong thinking.*

A person does not crucify himself. The drastic deed is
done by another. We do not crucify ourselves to the world
around us. God in Christ does this for us. By the principle of
dying daily to self, by dying to the subtle environmental
world influences at work on us, we are crucified, cut off to
them and they to us. (Read Romans 6.)

The moment a man is crucified he is set free from and delivered out of the environment in which he formerly existed.
The moment I am crucified to the world, to sin, to selfish interests I am set free (resurrected) into a new environment
and dimension of living, thinking, behaving, free to serve
God in that particular area of life.

This is an ongoing principle. It is an ongoing process. Our
thoughts, our minds, our interests can be set free from the
muddy thinking and sinister sinfulness of society. We can be
unshackled to set our minds on the shining splendor of
God's character instead of our silly little selves. We can have
our gaze shifted and lifted from the muck and mud of
human depravity to the scintillating Morning Star—Christ
our God.

Our focus can be on God our Father, shifted from the
vanity of man.

6) *Switching tracks in our thinking.*

God Our Father calls us to walk above the world. We are
invited to a holy, wholesome, and high-quality life with

Him. That does not mean that we are to live aloof, apart from, and indifferent to the suffering and sorrow of our broken world.

Rather Christ calls us to walk with Him in simplicity and sincerity, sensitive to the suffering of fellow pilgrims on the path. He calls us to be in the world, but not of it. He sends us to succor and save lost souls out of the mud and morass of human madness.

Only those with right thinking, godly attitudes, and Christlike compulsion can achieve His purposes on the planet. Our thinking must be switched from selfish pursuits to the Saviour's compassion and concern for the lost.

Our minds must be switched from the sordid and scandalous to the sublime and spiritual. We must pass from having our preoccupation with that which passes away to those values which are eternal and enduring (Philippians 4).

7) *The powerful impact of Christ's presence.*

We become like those with whom we associate. If we walk with worldlings, we will become like the world. If we walk in the counsel of the ungodly, or stand in sympathy with skeptics, or sit in company with cynics, our minds will be molded in that manner.

Blessed is the man that walketh not in the counsel of the ungodly, nor standeth in the way of sinners, nor sitteth in the seat of the scornful. But his delight is in the law of the Lord; and in his law doth he meditate day and night.

Psalms 1:1, 2

But the person who will spend time in God's Word, who will allow the gracious influence of God's Spirit to play upon his life, will be surprised at what happens. Give God some of your time and attention each day. Commune with Christ. Contemplate His character. Concentrate on His teaching. Meditate over His marvelous life. Share sweet moments speaking to Him. Cultivate His company. Relish His presence.

The impact of His life will radically alter your whole outlook on life. Gradually, gently, graciously, you will come to have the mind of Christ. You will walk with Him in noble thought.

2
Walking With God in My Emotions

Confusion in Christian Circles About Emotions

When we come to deal with the realm of human emotions and their role in our walk with God, we find ourselves caught up in very conflicting views. There are those who are convinced that Christianity is in large measure a highly charged emotional experience. They feel sure that the measure of their devotion to the Master is the extent to which they are moved emotionally.

On the other hand, there are those who tend to decry the emphasis on feelings in our relationship to God. They insist that our motivation must be grounded only in God's Word. They contend that our walk with Christ comes only by implicit faith in Him and His Word.

To help us come to clear and unclouded conclusions in this confusion, I wish to step back to some of the previous points made in this book. First it was pointed out that when God, by His gracious Spirit, begins to do a deep work of regeneration, remaking a person, He begins with the spirit of man. He touches us in the realms of our intuition, our conscience, and our capacity to commune with Him.

Often God has begun this inner work long before we may even be acutely aware of it either mentally or emotionally. All of His advances and overtures to us in the initial stages may well be a profound inner stirring of our spirit. This is often characterized by a certain unease—an inner awareness that somehow we are lacking something—there is a deep disquiet about life—a void or vacuum at the center of our being makes itself felt—we may be aware we are "missing the mark" in life—there is a lack of fulfillment, purpose, or direction to our days.

This impress of God's Spirit on our spirits cannot be grasped by the unregenerate mind of man. Nor can it be measured or gauged by purely human emotion. Even when we might wish to pray about it, we often do not know how, except in profound inner longings that cannot be articulated in human language.

The Need to Be Converted in Our Emotions

But as we are born again; as we begin to draw our new life from God; as we commune with Christ; as we come under the sovereignty of His Spirit, He does move upon our minds and emotions. He, the very Spirit of the Eternal God, does deal with us in both our thought-life and emotional experiences.

Put another way, God's Spirit gradually extends His sphere of influence beyond the realm of my spirit into the region of my soul. He does want to take new territory both in my thinking and in my sensations and ultimately, as we shall see in the next chapter, in my *will*.

As was pointed out in our discussion of the mind, we simply have to be converted in our thinking as Christians. Our thought patterns have to be conformed to those of Christ if we are to walk with Him in harmony. We have to have the mind of God in all matters that pertain to life.

Likewise in the realm of our emotions. These can no longer be allowed to tyrannize us. We are not people of childish, fickle moods, shunted about by our unpredictable and fragile feelings. We are not petty pawns pushed and pulled about on the chessboard of life by the whim of our emotional responses to the world around us.

We are not, if we intend to go places with God, people swept hither and thither by every wave of sentiment or changing tide of circumstance that washes around us. Instead we become strong, serene, stable souls with disciplined minds, disciplined emotions, and disciplined wills. We are determined to do God's will, and work, in a wretched world in spite of all the turmoil around us.

Just because we are surrounded by a society whose motto more and more becomes, "If it feels good, then do it!" does not mean we subscribe to that false and destructive philosophy. Ours is a hedonistic society, "high" on all that is sensual, soft, sentimental, and sinful. This may be the world's life-style but it is not ours.

The Distinction of Doing God's Will— Not Just What We Feel Like Doing

Increasingly the mark of true discipleship to the Master must be our willingness to part ways with the world when it comes to soulish, sensual, sentimental self-indulgence. We simply are not walking with God if we only *do what we feel like, when we feel like it, in the way we feel.*

Literally thousands of so-called Christians live their lives this way. They know absolutely nothing about behaving in a mature and disciplined way under the control of Christ. The whole idea and concept of being subject to the supreme sovereignty of God's Spirit is not only foreign to their feelings but actually abhorrent. In fact they flauntingly fling off any restraints which may be placed upon them, insisting that they have been set free in the spirit to do their own deplorable thing—whatever it may be they feel like doing.

This emphasis upon emotional experiences has become a fad in some circles. The tendency to stimulate and arouse soulish, sensual, sentimental sensations has swept up thousands of souls into a false sense of superspirituality. Their basis for believing that they are walking with God is grounded in the extent of their ecstatic experiences. Rather the true gauge of knowing God, loving Christ, and walking with Him in humility is the extent to which I do His will in a wicked world, whether or not I feel like it.

Please do not misunderstand what has just been said. This is not to advocate a cold, clinical, walk with God. If you have read this far in the book, you will know that is not meant at all. You will be fully aware that to walk with Christ entails communion with Him at the most profound and intimate levels of human experience.

Where the difficulty lies is that far too many of God's people are preoccupied with their feelings and experiences. Their focus is self-centered on their sensual selves, rather

than on the sublime and impeccable character of Christ.
Their sensations mean more to them than the Saviour Himself.

The person whose emotions are under Christ's control
becomes a powerful force for God in the world. In every life
they touch the Spirit uses their emotions to make an impact
for good.

Emotions Are Noble, Powerful, Appropriate, in Their Proper Place and Time

God's intention for His people is that their emotions and
feelings should be a great power for achieving His purposes
on the planet. Our feelings were never ever intended to
complicate or confuse us.

God Himself experiences enormous emotions.

His self-revelation to us is that He is touched with the
feelings of our infirmities (Hebrews 1, 2, 3, 4).

He is the God of peace.

He is the God of joy.

He is the God of sorrow.

He is the God of compassion.

He is the God of mercy.

He is the God of grief.

He is the God of righteous indignation.

He is the God of laughter and goodwill.

He made us in His own image. He created us in His own
likeness. He endowed us with the same capacity to experience and express emotion as He has.

Our emotions are and can be noble, powerful, gracious

gifts bestowed upon us by a generous Heavenly Father to not only enrich our own lives but also to bless others all around us. We hold in ourselves the capacity to contribute to the health, happiness, and well-being of our world.

The secret is, there is a proper time and place for each.

The Word of God brings this home to us with enormous impact in these simple statements:

To every thing there is a season, and a time to every purpose under the heaven: A time to be born, and a time to die; a time to plant, and a time to pluck up that which is planted; A time to kill, and a time to heal; a time to break down, and a time to build up; A time to weep, and a time to laugh; a time to mourn, and a time to dance; A time to cast away stones, and a time to gather stones together; a time to embrace, and a time to refrain from embracing; A time to get, and a time to lose; a time to keep, and a time to cast away; A time to rend, and a time to sew; a time to keep silence, and a time to speak; A time to love, and a time to hate; a time of war, and a time of peace.

Ecclesiastes 3:1–8

As we walk quietly, humbly with our God through a troubled, tangled world in turmoil, we become closely integrated and identified with His interests in it. We see as He sees. We feel as He feels. We respond as He responds.

We weep with those who weep. We laugh with those who laugh. We share in the sum total of the human story.

To Walk With God in My Emotions Is to Be Governed by God in My Behavior

It is an unmistakable mark of the man and woman moving in close communion with Christ that their emotions are governed not by self-interest, but by God. In their actions and reactions with others, the overriding desire and consideration is for the benefit and welfare of others. They have passed the point where they feel they were put on the planet just to please themselves.

Their relationships with other people, whether in a group or singly, is motivated not by self-indulgence but rather with the desire to enrich and bless others. They do not participate in emotional experiences at the expense of others in order to enhance their own egos. They do not exploit another person to promote their own ends.

In the world, amid a cynical society apart from God, social relationships are so often pursued for selfish, often sordid ends. Men and women play false and cruel games with one another in the name of love, friendship, or camaraderie. Yet all the time they are actually exploiting, impoverishing, and bewildering one another in lust, greed, and cruel cynicism.

The person who is walking with God in his emotions simply dares not indulge in such duplicity. We are God's people. We are governed by His behavior standards. We are sincere, honest, open, and genuine. If we are Christ's friend we do not fool around with the feelings of others. We do not capitalize on their capacity to reciprocate our advances. We simply do not take advantage of them. We do not give, in order to get.

If I am walking with God's Spirit as my constant companion and counselor, I shall have compassion, concern, and a genuine care for others as He does. This is to love my neighbor (anyone who crosses my path in life) as I love myself. I shall make no emotional move that adds to his load in life. Instead I shall endeavor to help him bear his burden with greater joy and a lighter step.

We Are Not to Be Manipulated by Either Our Moods or Mob Instincts

I have written at great length about our mental and emotional life in my book *Taming Tension*. Very practical but potent suggestions have been given there on how to handle those areas of our attitudes and feelings which lead to enormous tension and strain in our sophisticated society. So there is no need to go over all that ground again in this book.

But I do wish to touch on two very important points which perplex God's dear people in their walk with Him. The first of these is our predilection to undergo various moods. Moods have their roots in assorted causes, which if understood, will help us grapple with them. Amongst these are a) climatic changes, the rise and fall of barometric pressures; b) the state of our health, our physical and psychological cycles in our makeup; c) the rise and fall of circumstances and events in our personal affairs; d) the environmental influences of our surroundings and society.

A person can allow himself to be victimized by moods or he can surmount them. Oswald Chambers, in his straightforward, powerful manner, simply says: "You kick your moods!" You do not vent them on the innocent people around you who are not responsible for them.

Second, there is the matter of being manipulated by the mob instinct. Just because everyone does it never makes it right. We are called to be different, distinct people who walk with God. We are expected to be so controlled by Christ, so constrained by His Spirit, that we move in a totally different direction from the world.

We do not subscribe to its standards. We are not molded or compressed into its pattern of behavior. We move in a new dimension of life, energized and enlightened by the dynamic power of God's gracious Spirit—not the spirit of the world.

Experiencing and Expressing the Very Life and Love of God in Our Emotions (the Fruits of the Spirit)

It should by now be patently clear to the reader that, if we are in very truth born of God from above, then obviously our behavior has to be of a different sort from that of the world in which we live. If in fact we are walking hand in hand with Christ, our conduct must be of a unique caliber distinct from our contemporaries. If indeed the Spirit of God resides with us, our disposition of will, attitudes of mind, and emotional responses are bound to reflect His.

This is the only manner in which the men and women around us will ever be sure that we are the Christians we claim to be. To put it in very blunt terms, "Our lives speak so loudly that others often cannot hear what we have to say." And a very large part of the impact of our persons is made through the emotions we exhibit.

Using scriptural language we look for the fruits of God's own Spirit in the life of others. This is the positive evidence that in actual life we are what we claim to be, namely God's people, walking with Him in His way. I have written a whole book on this theme entitled *A Gardener Looks at the Fruits of the Spirit.* So there is no point in going over that ground again here.

It must be said, however, that if we are in harmony with God's Spirit, His life will be expressed through us in wholesome, healthy, helpful emotions. The joy, contentment, goodness, and other attributes of God Himself will emanate from us. The character and conduct of Christ Himself will be exemplified in our daily experiences. The close encounters and personal interrelationships we have with others will be an enormous blessing of rich benefit to them.

This is not because we are great or special people, but because we are walking in close communion with a great God. It is the impress of His life upon us and through us which makes an impact on others. It is the presence of His person which proves a blessing. His very life is being expressed and poured out through our emotions to a weary old world.

Several Simple Steps to Having Healthy Emotions

1) *Deliberately avoid degrading influences.*

There is abroad the peculiar notion that to avoid degrading and damaging worldly influences is a negative way to live. This simply is not so. The opposite is true. It takes deep convictions; concerted courage; strong faith in God, to step out strongly against the perverse practices of our soft, self-indulgent society. It calls for grit and gumption and godly fortitude to walk with God against the downward drift of a decadent culture.

Too many Christians are caught up in the syrupy, sentimental, syndrome of spurious love. They are too ready and eager to appear accommodating, soft, and easily led. As God's people we have to be prepared to walk a different path from the broad road of self-destruction upon which so many of our associates have set their feet. We have to be ready to declare fearlessly, "That way lies death—this way there is life!" We must be ready to cry out clearly, "That is evil, this is good!" not because we are pious prudes but because we are walking with God in a clear conscience, our souls enlightened by His presence, through His Word.

We cannot be manipulated by the mass mind. We refuse to allow our five senses (physical), which transmit to us stimuli from the world, to dominate our moods and emotions. We take a tough stand against what just makes us feel good. Instead we put God's will as paramount in our priorities. We determine to follow Christ no matter what it costs. We sever, in earnest, any and all contacts which would induce us to do wrong. We do not indulge our emotions, we invest our energies in God's purposes. (Read 2 Timothy 3.)

2) *Fling yourself wholeheartedly into God's work.*

The expression of emotion represents an enormous output of energy. It is a tragedy of the first magnitude that, for most people, this energy is wasted, lost like rocket fuel burned off aimlessly in the air, rather than propelling a spaceship to the stars.

God's intention for you and me is that our emotional en-

ergies will be directed and channeled into powerful purposes. He has work for us to do in the world. He has ambitions, aims, and aspirations for you to achieve. Discover
what they are. Get moving in harmony with His plan for
you. Fling yourself wholeheartedly into a cause for Christ
that is much greater than the cramped circumference of
your little life.

You were made for great ends. God our Father calls us to
glorious achievements. Don't be content with wasting your
pent-up emotional energies on your selfish self-interests. Set
your sights upon the bright and morning Star, your Saviour,
your Master, your Friend. Say to Him, "Whatever You
wish—I'll do it!"

He will energize your emotions. He will give them direction. He will provide the tremendous thrust by His Spirit
to get you off the old stale ground of self-centered preoccupation with your petty problems. He will send you on a life
mission, where the reoriented movement of your emotions
will be expended for others and for Him. He will use you to
achieve amazing missions. He will see to it that, as you move
and walk and commune with Him, your little life will make
an impact far beyond the narrow boundaries of your fragile
body and your few brief years upon the planet. (Read all of
Colossians and Philippians.)

You will have made a mark in the annals of eternity.

3) *Learn to "switch tracks" in your moods and emotions.*

For too many years, and for too many of us, it has been
true to say that we are a stale, stuffy, spineless people. The
time has come in the Western world (so-called Christian)
when we, as God's people, become marked men and women.

The distinctive "mark of the Master" must be upon us. We are different because of our disciplined lives, our disciplined minds, our disciplined emotions. We are people walking with God, doing His will.

His will is not for us to wallow around in the old mud holes of muddled thinking. It is not to be bogged down in the bestial behavior of a corrupt, rotten culture. It is not to have the mind-set of a materialistic society. It is not to indulge ourselves in old grievances; hostile grudges; angry animosities; hostile attitudes of hate and despair; jealous rage or selfish self-pity.

These and a thousand other damaging, destructive emotions have no part in our performance. God by His Spirit calls us to jettison this junk from the knapsacks on our backs. We are to travel light. We are to travel swiftly, surely, on the high road of wholesome, healthy, holy emotions. Get rid of the garbage—bury it in the ground of God's forgiveness. Move onto a high plane of lofty thought and noble living.

Get into good music; fine art; lofty literature; wholesome thinking in company with other zealous, keen, energetic Christians. There is a tremendous challenge to be moving with God's Spirit into exciting adventures of worthwhile endeavor. Let Him lead you into new enterprises. (Read Philippians 4 and all of Ephesians.)

4) *Cultivate the awareness of God's presence.*

It is the Christian who is acutely aware ("Oh, Christ, you are here!") whose emotions will be under God's control. He will know there is an appropriate time; a proper place; a fitting way in which his every emotion can be used for God.

There will be a moment to mourn; a moment to laugh; an

hour to be merry; a day to be white-hot with righteous anger for injustice done or evil perpetrated.

Be sensitive to God's Spirit within you. He will guide your energies. He will motivate you. He will manage your emotions. He will moderate your moods. He will generate the dynamic thrust that will make you a power for good.

You can be God's person in His place for His purposes.

Ask Him often, earnestly, quietly, "Oh, my Father, let me relish Your presence this hour in every emotion that engulfs me!" He will. Focus your faith on His wondrous person. He will be so pleased!

5) *Beseech God, in Christ, by His Spirit to literally flood your being with His life.*

It is this very life of the risen Christ, which is also the very love of the living God, which can be shed abroad in full measure in our souls by the Holy Spirit (Romans 5:5).

As this happens the very cleansing, changing, re-creative character of Christ replaces our old nature with His own wondrous new nature. His emotions (fruits of His Spirit) are then expressed to those around us.

The surging, shining, sparkling presence of His presence sweeps away our old, stale selfishness. Instead of being just filled with ourselves and selfish interests, our beings abound with His benefits that pour out from us in blessings to others.

An ancient legend recounts how the giant Hercules could not cleanse the huge Aegean stables of their accumulated dung deposited by thousands of horses for so many years. In a flash of inspiration Hercules went into the mountains. He found a sparkling glacial stream. With care, he diverted its course down the hills and through the stinking stables. In short order they were cleansed and swept clean by the flushing, flooding action of the sparkling stream.

Allow God's gracious Spirit in the same way to sweep into your sordid, soiled, soulish emotions. Soon He will cleanse, refresh, and remake you. Then out of you will flow streams of benefit to the ends of the earth.

3

Walking With God in My Will

General Remarks on the Will

At the beginning of this second section of the book, it was pointed out our souls are made up of our minds, our emotions, and our wills. Each has a tremendously important, significant role to play. Yet it is true to say that, unless in fact God governs my will, bringing it under control to Christ, subject to the sovereignty of His Holy Spirit, I can be a derelict drifting aimlessly. I shall not be a person walking with God.

For the greater part of the first half of this century, Christendom was caught up in intellectual theology. Christian dogma and teaching was directed largely to the mind of man. We were urged to consider God's Word more or less on an intellectual basis of understanding. The emphasis was that God had articulated Himself in a manner that man could apprehend almost exclusively with his mind.

The result was that many people came to "believe" in God in an intellectual dimension. The teachings of Christ were often set in the context of a code of ethics. A creed was emphasized for the churchgoer to subscribe to mentally.

Consequently many Christians were rather cold, clinical, and casual in their walk with God.

The second half of the century has seen a strong reaction to all of this. Throughout the world there has been a pronounced swing of the pendulum toward teaching which emphasizes experiences of a highly charged emotional nature.

Today there are great multitudes of sincere men and women for whom the sum total of their walk with God is an exciting, ecstatic, emotional sequence of experiences. They continually seek for satisfaction in an ongoing atmosphere of dramatic events, stimulating meetings, and supposedly spiritual "miracles."

Unfortunately for many of these people, they have been swept up in spurious teaching, not deeply grounded in God's Word. They have been allowed to believe that emotional and ecstatic experiences are the ultimate criteria for a Christian. They feel that they have attained a liberty of spirit which gives them license to live in a loose way. The net result has been to produce a whole generation more preoccupied with sensationalism and sensuality than with an obedient and humble walk with God.

Both for the church of Christ as a whole, and for the Christian as an individual, it simply is not enough to be either just an intellectual "believer" or an emotional "convert." The whole soul must be saved. The will must be touched, turned around, and transformed by the invasion and impact of God's Spirit.

There are thousands upon thousands of dear people who claim to be "born again" through either some intellectual assent or emotional experience. Yet their character and conduct is a direct denial of God's will. They may be active in church affairs, they may be in positions of leadership, but because their wills have never capitulated to Christ, there has never been any significant, deep, profound change in their persons.

This explains why apparently large crowds may seem to make decisions for Christ during great conventions or large evangelistic campaigns. Yet later, only a tiny remnant remain steadfast.

If a man is going to walk with God in harmony, in oneness, in complete accord, then his will must be brought into subjection to the will of God. The time has come when the church must realize this if it is to prosper.

What the Will Is

The simple word *will*, used here as a noun, is that capacity bestowed upon man by God to make profound choices. It is the faculty of his soul that makes decisions. It is the central citadel of his person where he determines to do what he wants—to be what he wishes—to go where he desires. It is his volition!

The will is my innermost *self*.

It really is my control center—*me—I—mine.*

It is seldom referred to in the Scriptures as the *"will"*—instead it is called *"the heart of man."*

Many preachers, teachers, and scholars assume that, when the Word of God speaks of the heart, it is referring to the seat of our emotions. Not so! The will of a man is the heart of a man's decision-making capacity.

There is much confusion about the term *heart* in God's Word. A note of explanation may help the reader here.

Heart is an Anglo-Saxon word used to describe the powerful organ which pumps blood through our bodies and thus maintains life. It was always considered the most important part of the entire body. It was essential to life itself. It was, in fact, looked upon as the very center of the body's being, upon which all else depended.

In time the term *heart* began to be used for anything absolutely central and essential. For example, a common phrase we now use is "That is the heart of the matter," meaning that is the central issue—the very essence to the whole problem.

Likewise, we may speak of "the heart of a tree," meaning the central, hard, tough wood in the center of the tree surrounded by the softer outer layers with their covering of bark.

Similarly, in dealing with the heart of man, the Word of God is referring explicitly to that tough, hard, inner core of self, surrounded by its swathing of mind and emotions. This inner will, this inner self, this inner heart, must be changed if a man is to walk with God.

Setting the Will

Not only does the will act in making choices and decisions, but even more importantly it actually determines under God our ultimate destiny. This is a most sobering realization.

God is a freewill being. When He made man in His own wondrous image, He endowed him, too, with a will which was free to be set in different directions. Either man could set his will to walk with God or to flee from God. He could choose to do God's will or he could decide to do his own will.

Essentially the whole sad, tragic report given to us of Adam and Eve in the magnificent environment of Eden is a divine commentary on man setting his will to walk in his own way rather than choosing to walk with God in His way.

So powerful, so profound, so potent is the will that a child who sets his will at an early age to become a certain person is bound to achieve his end. The will, once set on a certain goal, is like a gyroscope set on the polestar. Nothing will shift its direction.

Show me a person who sets his will with steel-like determination, and I will show you a person who is invincible and irresistible. Absolutely nothing can deter him from his aim. Nothing can divert him from achieving his ambition. Nothing can deflect his decision to be what he wishes, to do what he wants, to go where he will.

Christians simply are not challenged enough to set their wills to serve Christ; to follow Him at any cost; to walk with Him in close communion. Too many of us drift along dreamily, with no special aim to walk with God; no deep, driving desire to do His will; no steel-like determination to be aligned with His wishes and work in the world. Our Christianity is often only a cozy, comfortable, casual social function that we engage in for food, fun, and fellowship.

It was Joshua of old, my second greatest hero in the Bible, who declared fearlessly and unashamedly to his contemporaries: ". . . as for me and my house, we *will* serve the Lord" (Joshua 24:15). The rest of the crowd could choose to do what they wished, but nothing would deflect or deter this gallant general.

It was Elijah, the flaming prophet of fire, who challenged all of Israel on Mount Carmel with the ringing words, ". . . How long halt ye between two opinions? if the Lord be God, follow him: but if Baal, then follow him . . ." (1 Kings 18:21).

All through the record of God's dealing with the human race He comes to us, challenging us to set our wills. He uses every avenue of approach to get at this central citadel of our souls. Sometimes His Spirit appeals to us through our minds; sometimes through our emotions; sometimes through the impact of circumstances, events, or people about us. But always His ultimate goal is to capture the central citadel of our hearts, *our wills.*

Until this happens, really nothing changes either in our character or conduct. We may give intellectual assent to His revelation about Himself and ourselves; we may even become highly emotional about what we see; we may shed tears of self-pity or remorse; we may become highly agitated or excited temporarily, but unless our wills are touched, turned about, and attuned to His, nothing alters. We simply go on doing our own thing; living our same old life-style; indulging our own self-centered desires; walking in our own wretched, wicked ways.

We may try to delude ourselves into believing we are "born again"—we may think because we subscribe to a certain creed, or engage eagerly in ecstatic, emotional experiences that we are walking with God. But it is utter self-deception if still our wills are set against doing God's will. We can sing, pray, praise, perform miracles, and execute dramatic displays of supposed Christian service. But if we do not walk with God in our wills, it is all for naught.

The most solemn, searching, sobering statement Jesus Christ ever made on this matter is this:

> Not every one that saith unto me, Lord, Lord, shall enter into the kingdom of heaven; but he that doeth the will of my Father which is in heaven.

> Many will say to me in that day, Lord, Lord, have we not prophesied in thy name? and in thy name have cast out devils? and in thy name done many wonderful works?

> And then will I profess unto them, I never knew you: depart from me, ye that work iniquity.
>
> Matthew 7:21–23

It remains a melancholy mystery how men and women can set their wills for almost every other purpose in life, yet find it abhorrent to set their wills to walk with God. Of course, to a degree this does depend on how they have been instructed in God's Word. Too many are taught that they can just coast along cheerfully in an aura of semispirituality, where no deep discipline is demanded: that walking with God is merely a matter of having a nodding acquaintance with Christ. Setting our wills to serve God is much more than some sort of casual acquaintance. It is a devout determination to know and do God's will.

Bringing Our Wills Under God's Government

When our Lord was among us, He had one theme which He emphasized more than any other. It was the "Kingdom of God," referred to in Matthew's account as the "Kingdom of heaven." Unbeknown to most of His audience, and to His followers today, this theme is, at heart, the matter of man's will.

Christ used numerous parables to portray what the Kingdom of God was. He explained these parables to His disciples but even then they seemed not to understand. And until we grasp this concept, we, too, shall never understand what God's intentions are for our wills.

Let me explain. To have a kingdom you must have a king, a monarch, a sovereign. By the same definition, to have a kingdom you must have those in it who are subject to the sovereign. They are those who enjoy the benefits and protection of their monarch. Their lives are enriched because they allow themselves to be governed and ruled under a benign sovereignty.

The subjects subscribe to and endorse the will of their monarch by being loyal and obedient to Him. They recognize that the laws and edicts of their ruler are designed and drawn up with their own best interests in mind. They are contented citizens of a special community under the control of their own special sovereign. Gladly, cheerfully, wholeheartedly they choose of their own free will to be governed and ruled this way. Their king's will and wishes are their cherished commands, their very code of conduct. They willingly, gladly sacrifice their lives for king and country. It is a price they are prepared to pay for the remarkable privilege of living under his power.

This is the precise picture Christ endeavored to convey to His contemporaries. Few ever caught the vision. Few see it today.

Our God has established the Kingdom of heaven—or Kingdom of God—His Kingdom. He invites us to become citizens of that community. He extends an invitation to us to become Christians (Christ's men and women). He welcomes us to give our allegiance to Christ, the King of kings.

But, and it is a very big *but,* the conditions for becoming a part of that very unique and privileged community is that we shall be willing a) to be governed by God; b) to come under Christ's control; c) to be subject to the sovereignty of His Spirit.

In other words, the mainspring of my being, the central control of my person, the free will of my soul is brought into glad and harmonious agreement with God's intentions. To be subject to God's sovereignty is not to be a slave beaten down into sniveling servitude. Rather it is to be a "born again" son—a freeborn child—who willingly, joyously, gratefully chooses to be a citizen of heaven—a member of God's Kingdom—one who deliberately, freely chooses to come under Christ's control.

Such a soul has set his will to be governed by God, for he knows He has only his best interests in mind. He sets his will to be led and directed by God's sovereign Spirit. That way lies liberty, love, and life, keeping company with Christ.

Steps We Take to Align Our Wills With God's

1) *Discover and determine what His will is.*

In my book *A Layman Looks at the Lord's Prayer,* the entire matter of God's will has been dealt with at great length. There is no need to cover all that ground here again. However, several salient points must be made to help the reader.

The *will of God* is a term used to denote all of God's intentions, desires, wishes, and purposes for both this planet earth and the people on it. More specifically, *God's will* applies to those men and women who do respond in positive faith to Him, and who, in simple confidence and obedience, go on to commune and walk with Him.

Because of the impeccable and wondrous character of God, all of His will toward both the universe as a whole, and a single soul in particular, is good, desirable, just, kind, patient, loving, gracious, gentle, strong, and generous. Above all He is faithful, sincere, honest, and totally trustworthy by virtue of the fact that this is His very makeup. He cannot be otherwise. All His intentions toward us are desirable:

> For I know the thoughts that I think toward you, saith the Lord, thoughts of peace, and not of evil, to give you an expected end.
>
> Then shall ye call upon me, and ye shall go and pray unto me, and I will hearken unto you.
>
> And ye shall seek me, and find me, when ye shall search for me with all your heart [*will*].
>
> Jeremiah 29:11–13

Our simple responsibility is to get into God's Word, to ruminate in it, to revel in it, to rejoice and delight ourselves in discovering how great and good and generous His will is for us. We discover He has nothing but our best interests in mind. His heart is set only on our welfare. So we, too, come to want His will more than anything else. Our fiercest desire is that our wills be aligned with His will. Our joy and delight is to do His will and comply with His wishes. In all of this we show our genuine, honest love for Him. (Read John 14 and 15.)

The will of God streams and flows like a colossal, cosmic current through the seas of time. Only the person who also moves in accord with it finds purpose and direction in a divine destiny of utter fulfillment.

If you would walk with God in your will, discover what it is. Then do it! Step out in simple faith, your attention centered in Christ to go where He asks you to go; to live as He instructs you to live; to be what He asks you to be; to do what He asks you to do.

As you set your will to so live, you are taking the first giant step of faith which He will honor. He in turn will be faithful to you and empower you to walk with Him in joy.

For it is God which worketh in you both to will and to do of his good pleasure.

Philippians 2:13

2) *Focus your attention on Christ.*

When an ardent hiker heads for the high country, he keeps his eyes fastened on the far ridges and shining summit. He stimulates himself and steels his resolve to reach the top by focusing his attention on the ultimate goal.

If he has a traveling companion, a hiking partner, he will also give him much of his thought, time, and interest. By doing this, the obstacles and hardships and strain of the climb are scarcely noticed. The tough, rough spots are taken in stride without undue stress or strain. His eyes and interest are not centered on the immediate problems along the path, but on reaching the mountaintop.

It is precisely the same in our walk with God. Where is your focal point of interest? Are you completely preoccupied with the petty pressures and problems of the immediate moment? Are you so taken up with self-interest that you can't see the shining heights of God's purposes and plan for the world? Is your gaze only on the ground of your grinding, grumbling, grievances, or does God Himself fill your view?

Learn to refocus your attention on Christ. Make Him your confidante. Keep Him always in view. Set your will deliberately to see and press on toward the destination of the high country and lofty life to which He has called you.

> Not as though I had already attained, either were already perfect: but I follow after, if that I may apprehend that for which also I am apprehended of Christ Jesus.
>
> Brethren, I count not myself to have apprehended: but this one thing I do, forgetting those things which are behind, and reaching forth unto those things which are before,
>
> I press toward the mark for the prize of the high calling of God in Christ Jesus.
>
> Philippians 3:12–14

Refuse to let reverses, frustrations, discouragements, or seeming disasters distract your attention from God's will for you. Pursue His purposes. Set your sights on His loftiest ideals and aspirations for you. Let nothing intrude between Him and you.

You can be a great achiever with God. You can climb the heights and reach otherwise impossible pinnacles. His inspiration, His companionship, His goodwill, His cheer, and hope are all there for you to revel in. But it is up to you to want to do this. It is up to you to choose with your will to reach the high country of noble living in company with Christ. These are your decisions. They are a definite, deliberate act of your will.

Invite God Himself by His Spirit to share your traveling days through this life's tangled trails. He will be glad to come. And your journey will be joyous.

3) *Let the impact of Christ's presence overcome the obstacles along the way.*

It would be despicable deception if I were to lead you to believe that walking with God is nothing but joy. It simply is not so. When He Himself was here among us, despite His perfect life and perfect character, He encountered all sorts of grief and hardship. His was a tough trail to tramp. He was the "man of sorrows" acquainted with grief. He was hated, despised, ridiculed, and abused. Yet He was also strong, serene, and of goodwill all the way.

He told His twelve companions, "In this world you will have tribulation: but be of good cheer; I have overcome the world" (*see* John 16:33). He also declared, "I am with you always, even to the end of this age" (*see* Matthew 28:20).

Deliberately, with a strong will, cultivate the companionship of Christ as you walk through this weary old world. "Oh, Christ, You are here. I shall take the tough trails of life as You take them. I shall triumph and overcome obstacles as You do!"

How? What is the secret?

By daily denying my own selfish desires, whims, and petty pride.

Let the same principle of death to self, crossing out the little petty priorities of my own person, put an end to my peevishness and petulance. This is the crossing out of my self-centered will in all its daily decisions. This is to have the "cross" of Christ, who is my Companion, become a powerful principle in the daily, hourly events of my life.

"Not my will, but Yours, Oh, Lord, be done here." Or, put another way, "Yes, Master, if that is the best way for us to go, then let's go!"

Walking this way with God in a submissive will is to have His power released in our experiences. God is set free to lead us along difficult but challenging trails. His Spirit is thrilled to take us over places we otherwise would have refused to go.

Don't buck God. Don't debate the way with Him. Put your hand in His; look up into His smiling face and simply say, "If that's best, let's do it together!"

4) *Just take one step at a time with God.*

God promised Joshua that every step he took, every spot where he set his foot down in quiet faith and simple obedience, would be given to him. (Read Joshua chapter 1 carefully.)

God does not ask you to climb the heights or cross the tough terrain in one giant leap. He knows you cannot. He asks you to take the journey with Him one step at a time.

By a definite, deliberate act of your will, decide to do the thing He asks you to do today; this hour; this moment. The instant you step out in quiet faith, to freely comply with His will, He empowers you to achieve His aims and ambitions for you.

Joshua stepped into the Jordan. God held back the river.

Joshua stepped out around Jericho. God flattened the walls.

Your part is to walk with God in unflinching faith, just one step at a time. His part is to prove faithful in performing everything He invites you to attempt. He always does. He cannot be unfaithful to Himself, to His Word, or to you.

Walk with Him unafraid; filled with confidence; quietly assured that it is He who can make your trip a triumph.

SECTION
III

WALKING WITH GOD IN MY BODY

CHAPTER

1
Walking With God
in My Bodily Drives

Our Bodies, God's Residence

Earlier in this book it was pointed out that when God's gracious Spirit touches our lives, He does so in very unobtrusive ways, beginning at the very center of our beings in the realm of our spirit. Gradually, as we go on walking with God, allowing Him to influence more and more of our life, His will is done in our souls; how we think; how we employ our emotions; how we decide with our wills.

But a last stronghold remains. It is the body. Almost like a formidable bastion, it is the area in which we so often are the least able to relinquish our drives, desires, and habits to Christ's control. The well-known British author Oswald Chambers, used so mightily of God at the beginning of this century, makes this point again and again in his books.

Many of God's very earnest people, who conscientiously walk with Him both in spirit and soul, seem to have a deep, inner reluctance to allow Christ control of their bodily behavior. They act almost as if this were a realm outside of and apart from His area of interest and influence. In part this is because they do not carefully examine God's Word on the matter.

To begin with, Scripture is surprisingly explicit in stating that our bodies are the temple (the residence) of the Holy Spirit. God does not only dwell among His people, the body of Christ (the church), but He actually occupies our bodies individually.

Paul put it to the carnal, sensual Christians at Corinth in this way:

> The body is not for licentiousness, but for the Lord, and the Lord is for the body.... or do you not know that your body is a sanctuary of the Holy Spirit within you—the Spirit whom you have from God?
>
> And you are not your own, for you have been bought at a price. Glorify [honor] God, then, in your bodies.
>
> 1 Corinthians 6:14, 19, 20 WEYMOUTH

When in quiet, serious, sober contemplation we come to this realization, it alters our attitudes toward bodily behavior and bodily care. When it dawns upon us at last that God is very much concerned with the bodily habits of mere man, it suddenly thrusts our physical conduct into a bright new light. We come to see that God is very much involved with the whole of life. He does not limit His interests only to our spirits and souls as so many naively and wrongly assume.

In large part, the reason for this must be laid at the doorstep of the preachers, teachers, and Christian scholars who so often engross themselves only with so-called spiritual issues, while totally neglecting or overlooking what God has to say about our bodies.

Yet there is a peculiar, human twist to all of this teaching and thinking. Namely, we often find that Christians are preoccupied with bodily sins and wrongdoing as though they are much more gross and offensive to God than the sins of the soul and spirit.

For example, in the estimation of most people, such wrong behavior as drunkenness or adultery is considered much more despicable than jealousy or bad temper. The former are looked upon as very evil and repugnant, whereas so often the latter are brushed aside as mere weaknesses of human frailty. In God's view, the two types may well be reversed in seriousness simply because we are sinning in ways which we do not consider serious, in a higher level of our person, nor in need of correction.

Amid all this confused thinking, very little guidance is given to lay people as to how to walk with God in their bodies. Leaders, preoccupied with the symptoms of bad bodily behavior, give very little practical advice on how to live and walk with God's Spirit in such a way that our bodies can be wholesome, noble, holy habitations for the Most High.

God calls us to honor Him with our bodies. He makes it clear that He is just as anxious to enter and exert His sovereignty there as anywhere else. So let us try and understand His instructions in this area and act on them with integrity as we walk with Him.

Bodily Drives and What They Are

Our physical bodies are characterized by powerful, compelling, insistent drives. In some scientific circles these are referred to as basic animal instincts. They are more or less the common denominator to all natural life upon the planet. From the lowest life forms of plant and animal organisms to the loftiest levels of Homo sapiens—man—imperative instincts drive the body to behave in certain ways.

There are innumerable drives, but three main ones totally dominate and overshadow all others. Here they are:

1) *The drive to take and hold territory.*

That is, to possess space, to establish a power base from which can be drawn or derived sufficient resources for:

2) *The extraction of sustenance and support sufficient to insure survival.*

In other words, there must be the means of insuring the continuation of life in order to:

3) *Reproduce and perpetuate the species upon the planet.*

This includes all the diverse means of sexual reproduction.

Putting it all into the plainest possible terms, we can say an animal organism demands and drives for:

1. territory, or a power base of possessions;
2. food, drink, and shelter derived from possessions; and,
3. sexual reproduction with the strength so gained.

Out of these basic drives arise innumerable desires, appetites, passions, and other lesser instincts far too numerous to list in this book.

Taking Territory—Gaining Ground: The Drive for Bodily Survival

It matters not whether it is a meadowlark, staking out his nesting territory in the spring, or a primitive tribe fighting for hunting territory in the Amazon jungles, or a modern business executive struggling to establish a power base in the concrete jungle of Chicago: all living organisms are engaged in this drive for possessing territory.

With the sophistication of modern Western society, the struggle to gain ground is not quite as obvious as a mountain tribesman in Burma clearing and burning a patch of forest where he can plant his rice. But the drive and thrust and instinct of survival is so intense that we in the West engage in education, science, the arts, modern technology, business, commerce, industry, careers of a hundred sorts to carve out and establish power bases for ourselves. These are masked and somewhat screened by the complexity of our society and the intricacies of our culture.

Still the fact remains that the well-dressed Westerner with his shining car and air-conditioned offices is using his bodily energy and instincts just as vehemently as the jungle man clad only in a loincloth hacking at the forest with a machete.

In short, we are all fighting to take territory. We are all out to gain ground. We are all intent on establishing a power base. We are all piling up possessions.

These possessions are not necessarily just material assets as so many assume in Christian circles. It is not just a preoccupation with mere materialism. It can be more than land, barns, furniture, houses, cars, or bank accounts. It can equally be careers, degrees, diplomas, technology, personal contacts, a whole host of intangible assets from which wealth may be drawn and derived in a thousand different ways.

From our infancy we are taught, trained, and told that this is the sure way to success. We are encouraged to carve out a power base that will insure survival. We are urged to use all of our bodily strength, energy, and activities to achieve these ends. *We simply must get ahead. We must gain ground.*

The net result is that we are people preoccupied with possessions. We are completely convinced that only in the abundance of things we own can there be assurance of survival. So we use our bodies as vehicles to attain these ends. They are considered entirely expendable for our own selfish, self-centered ambitions.

Jesus, when He was here, came to grips with this whole concept when He told the story of the very successful landowner who was absolutely sure he had it made with his enormous holdings and gigantic crops. (Read Luke 12:13–21 very carefully and prayerfully in several translations.)

You will notice that before pointing out the folly of the self-assured farmer, our Lord said very directly, ". . . a man's life consisteth not in the abundance of the things which he possesseth" (Luke 12:15).

Then He went on further to call the farmer a fool for feeling he was secure in the affluence which he enjoyed and reveled in so blatantly. He could lose it all overnight.

The basic issue was that he had used all of his bodily capacities to achieve a power base that could be lost. As Knox's translation sums it up, such is the status of a person who has expended all of his bodily energies for selfish, materialistic, personal ends without ever establishing any credit with God.

This raises sobering, searching questions. Is my body being used only in my own interests in life? Is it doing anything to achieve God's ends in the world? Is He being honored by my bodily behavior? Am I intent only on taking territory for myself, gaining ground for my power base, or are my physical activities adding to God's assets?

Where am I going with my body? What am I doing with my body? How am I using or abusing it? Do I see it as something to pander to my pride, to accumulate more personal possessions? Or do I see it as the residence of God Himself of which I am the caretaker and doorkeeper?

> For a day in thy courts is better than a thousand. I had rather be a doorkeeper in the house of my God, than to dwell in the tents of wickedness.
>
> Psalms 84:10

The Supply of Food, Drink, Clothing and Shelter: The Drive for Bodily Security and Support

Being what we are as human beings, endowed with physical bodies that require food, drink, air, shelter, exercise, sunshine and rest to flourish, these do demand our attention. It follows, too, that if we recognize the sanctity of our bodies as the residence of God's own Spirit, they do deserve proper care and maintenance. Our bodies are not ours to misuse or to abuse. We, too, are their residents. We owe them the proper respect and regard of a temporary tenant. They are entrusted to our care for the rather brief occupancy of our short sojourn on earth.

There have been in the past, and still are abroad today, some strange views held by certain Christians toward the body. It is almost held in contempt as essentially something evil. It is literally despised. There are ascetics who starve, abuse, and mutilate their bodies. Outside of Christendom, especially in the Oriental religions and pagan cults, the body is subjected to all sorts of flagellations.

At the other end of the spectrum there are people whose whole lives are spent and devoted to pandering to the body. They wrap all of their affection and attention around it. They spend enormous sums adorning it and dressing it. They spend hours of time each day in bodily care and beautification. They invest enormous energy and interest in bodily exercise and entertainment. They use a large share of their income to feed their bodies the finest fare, the most delectable drinks, and the most expensive sedatives or stimulants.

In short, it can be said that some focus all their interest on the body and its well-being.

To fulfill all its demands they draw upon all their resources. To satisfy their bodily preoccupation, most of their thought, energy, time, and strength is devoted to the support and sustenance of the body.

Our Lord knew all of this. He saw the sadhus who fasted and the fakirs who trod the dusty roads of His own land mutilate themselves in public displays of supposed piety. He knew, too, all about the inordinately wealthy upper class whose fabulous feasts and drinking bouts were a byword of His day. He had been a guest in some of those sumptuous homes.

All of this human drama, display, and debauchery He held up to view in His parables. He told the story of the rich man and the beggar Lazarus lying at his door. He told about the arrogant Pharisee and poor publican in their prayers. He gave the startling account of the wealthy farmer who said to himself, "Soul, thou hast much goods laid up for many years [absolute security]; take thine ease [relax]; eat, drink, and be merry [live it up, you've got it made]."

Yet that very night the whole scenario suddenly ended. It came to a catastrophic conclusion with just one stabbing, sobering, searching question from God Himself: "You fool! Who now benefits from all your bodily interest?" Standing stripped, the wretched fellow had never established any credit of eternal value with God. His total bodily preoccupation ultimately left him a pauper in eternal values (*see* Luke 12:16–21).

Our Lord then went on to warn us that though the world in its folly may feel justified in being preoccupied with bodily needs, we are not so to be. If in truth we are walking with Him in close association, we will be aware that our view of our bodies should be sane, sensible, and balanced.

Two principles for proper bodily care.

There are two simple, basic principles upon which a Christian walks with God in this area.

1. He recognizes that his Heavenly Father knows he has bodily needs. Just as He supplies for birds, grass, flowers, and trees so He provides for His people.

Most of us don't really believe this. Positive proof that we don't is the manner in which we eternally struggle, scheme, and scramble to meet those needs with our own resources.

They do occupy a priority place in our thinking and planning. Put in rather blunt language, most of us do not eat and drink and dress in order to live, and so serve God. Rather we live to eat and drink and dress to satisfy ourselves and impress others. Our priorities are completely reversed.

We do not and cannot walk with God that way.

Our bodily pride is our passion. And against such God sets Himself. It is a sobering reflection.

The path of peace in this area of our bodies is to recognize in genuine humility, "Oh, God, You brought me into being! Oh, God, You will and do supply my needs—all good gifts come from Your generous hand. Oh, God, gladly, cheerfully, I accept Your provision for me. It is plenty; it is abundant. It will be used to keep my body, Your body, fit, well and vigorous, for both our sakes. And together, in joint residence, we will work and live and rejoice together in blessing a broken world."

2. The second great principle for bodily well-being has been enunciated by Christ in the compelling statement, "Seek ye first the kingdom of God, and his righteousness; and all these things shall be added unto you" (Matthew 6:33; *see also* Luke 12:31).

Again it must be said that most of us don't really believe this. We simply are not sure it can be so.

A lifetime of conditioning convinces us to the contrary. We are sure the only source of security is to pile up our own possessions, accumulate our own resources, store up our own supplies in such abundance that there will be enough to last us all our days.

This was the way I lived until I was forty-seven years old. I then owned a magnificent mountain ranch in the warm, sunny, beautiful lake country of southern British Columbia.

I had nearly a thousand acres of excellent land. It was graced with beautiful forest trees, lush stream bottoms, and open parkland.

The property encircled a lovely, secluded lake. Clear mountain streams cascaded through the valley. Eleven mountain springs fed these streams. There was peace, plenty, privacy. What more could a man want in a busy, boisterous world? Deer and upland birds roamed the hills. Trout flashed through the water.

One day God put His hand upon my land and asked me in unmistakable language: "Phillip, what is first in your affection—this magnificent property or Me? Are you prepared to give it all away to bless others? Do you really believe I can care for you without this power base, without these resources to meet your bodily needs?"

For months I was in anguish of soul and spirit. I really did not believe He could. Finally in trembling, faltering, child-like confidence, I complied with His request. I gave it all away freely to serve others of His dear people.

The subsequent fourteen years God in turn has poured into my life a continuous abundance. From sources unknown and unexpected He has sent all that was ever needed to meet my bodily requirements. He has filled my life full and overflowing with bodily bounties.

You see, these books I write are not theory. They are not doctrine. They come from the tough trails God and I have tramped together across the years.

Put God first and He will insure your bodily needs, whatever they be. Walk with Him in the beauty of simple trust.

Sexual satisfaction.

So many books, pamphlets, and papers on sex have flooded the field of Christian literature in recent years that I do not wish to elaborate further on the subject here. My views on this have been stated simply but forthrightly in the book *Taming Tension*.

Sufficient to say here that sexual activity is essentially God's intention for us. It is of His design and origin for the perpetuation of the human race.

Within the framework of the family and in company with a true life companion to whom one is devoted, loyal, and faithful, sex can be:

BEAUTIFUL—NOT BESTIAL
NOBLE—NOT DEGRADING
PRECIOUS—NOT PERVERTED
SUBLIME—NOT SORDID
SATISFYING—NOT FRUSTRATING

The Word of God abounds with clear, concise commands as to how we should behave in sexual relationships. Our bodies, being the residences of God, are not ours to abuse or misuse. When we come together with our mate, there are three persons in close communion, not just two, for God Himself is also present by His Spirit.

This awareness does not deter us from deep delight. Rather it stimulates and inspires us with its divine dimension of dignity and spiritual uplift. What we enjoy, we enjoy openly and confidently and joyously, joined to one another and joined to God Himself.

The world's sordid, low view of sex is that at best it is little more than a physical activity with certain emotional overtones. God's view is that it is a function embracing the whole of man: body, soul, and spirit. It is, within the family of God, an exhilarating, enobling, reassuring part of our bodily behavior upon which God places special blessings and benefits. As we comply with His wishes in this area He, too, rejoices to share it with us: "Now the body is not for fornication [licentiousness] but for the Lord, and the Lord is for the body" (1 Corinthians 6:13 WEYMOUTH).

Sex is not something to be ashamed of in our walk with God. Rather it can be exceedingly enobling, comforting, and strengthening.

Our bodies are not ours to indulge in fornication whether in fact, fancy, or fantasy. We are not given those prerogatives as God's people. We are called to purity.

We are given the responsibility to reproduce ourselves; to rejoice in the love of a true life mate; to render great honor to God's Spirit who is a participant with us in this noble function.

The sneering world may label us "puritans." It is a name we should be glad to bear. For we can be a wholesome, healthy, holy people—not polluted or perverted by a promiscuous, perishing society that applauds licentiousness in the name of "liberty." That way lies enslavement to selfish lust. In God's way there lies freedom from all fear, for perfect love dispels fear. (Read 1 John.)

2

Walking With God in My Bodily Desires

The Source of Bodily Desires

Any man, any woman, any child who has ever had a deep, inner longing to walk with God in close and sweet communion knows the stress and tension produced by his/her bodily desires. These powerful appetites and passions have posed an enormous problem. Too often they have been the area of enormous turmoil, titanic temptation, and tragic tension alienating God and man.

The biographies of God's greatest men and loveliest women are replete with the struggle to deal with desire. The constant ferment and fever of our few short years of life on the planet are inexorably bound up with the insatiable (supposedly) appetites and passions of our bodies.

The cries which have come from some of God's choicest saints show the severity of struggle that has engulfed them. They are echoed again and again by Christians of every generation. Here are several heart cries!

My God, I wish to give myself to thee. Give me the courage to do so. Strengthen my feeble will which sighs for thee. I stretch my arms to thee! ... Lead me after

thee by the bonds of thy love. Lord, whose am I, if not
thine own? What hard bondage to belong to myself and
to my passions!

FENELON

Have mercy upon me, O God, according to thy loving kindness . . . blot out my transgressions. Wash me
thoroughly from mine iniquity and cleanse me from my
sin. For I acknowledge my transgressions: and my sin is
ever before me!

DAVID (after his affair with Bathsheba)

If such deep-seated longings for deliverance from bodily
desires are wrung in agony from those of us who yearn to
walk with God in harmony, we must understand their
source.

Please reflect seriously a moment on the three major bodily drives mentioned in the preceding chapter:

Out of the drive for taking territory, for gaining ground,
for establishing a power base that we feel guarantees survival, there are generated desires for possessions, prestige,
power, and pride of place.

Out of the basic bodily drive for eating, drinking, cloth-
ing, and shelter to support and sustain us, there comes a host
of appetites, tastes, and powerful personal preferences.

Out of the bodily drive to reproduce the race and indulge
in sexual relationships, there arise impassioned desires not
only for physical intercourse but also self-aggrandizement in
luxury, ease, and sensual passions.

The net result is that we are caught up in, and carried
along by, an endless, feverish, frantic discontent. We search;
we seek; we strive; we struggle to satisfy our bodily desires.
We become driven people. We are enmeshed and enslaved
by our desires, yet know it not.

How We Are Exploited and Manipulated in Our Desires

The tragic, terrifying truth is that not only are we aware of our intense bodily appetites, passions, and desires, but so, too, is the world (society apart from God) and Satan (the god of this world), the enemy of our lives. These forces will do anything to inflame, arouse, and further distract us, to deflect us from our walk with Christ in close communion.

They use any and every means at their disposal to disrupt our harmony with God. They will so manipulate and exploit and stimulate our bodily desires that we are distracted from God's company. Our passions intrude between us and Him. They love to lead us down the broad road of self-satisfaction and self-indulgence to ultimate self-destruction. We simply must see this.

1. The Demands of a Hedonistic Society

We live in a hedonistic period of history. We in the Western world, which is Christian in name only, have really given rise to a heathen, hedonistic culture. We are completely committed to pleasure, leisure, and luxury. Our society, said to have the highest standard of living in the world, is rich in material aspects, which pander to our passions, but leave us impoverished in our spirits.

Our primary preoccupation is not with God's work in the world, but with our own selfish self-interests. The priorities which are uppermost in Christ's economy simply do not rate in our value systems. Evidence of this can be found in our entire educational system.

God is not even taken into consideration. His views, His wishes, His standards, His interests, His values are not even given minimal consideration in the school curriculum. Children are completely and totally oriented to materialistic, hedonistic ideologies.

The ultimate aim of education is not to know God, but rather to *know yourself and realize all your own desires.* From earliest infancy, children are not encouraged to learn to walk with God but rather to learn how to walk in the world's ways.

To a very great extent this implies that the young person, through no fault of his/her own, absorbs and acquires a value system, a set of priorities, diametrically opposed to those of God in Christ.

The main criterion of success in our society is not to be still and quiet and content in the company of Christ. Rather it is to be the person on the go, struggling, searching, seeking frantically to fulfill himself by self-gratification. Amass wealth, pile up possessions, establish a power base, eat, drink, luxuriate, take your ease, satisfy every desire, pander to every passion.

In the process we ignore God completely.

2. *The Insidious Stimulation of Business and Industry*

It is indeed difficult for those who have grown up in the Western world to realize the extent to which they are actually manipulated by business and industry. Our whole economic process is predicated upon the principle of supply and demand. Therefore the supplier simply must create demand if he is to survive.

Those of us who have grown up in a much more simple society stand back stunned and shocked by the plethora of products produced and pedaled to the public in the name of good business. Hundreds of thousands of articles are offered for sale with the most lavish advertising and packaging.

People are led to believe that they simply must have these products. They are convinced that as consumers their needs are absolute necessities. The upshot is that we are tempted and titillated to purchase and possess a wide variety of items, not one of which may do anything but indulge further our sensuality.

Commerce and advertising direct their drives at our bodily desires; our tastes; our appetites; our personal passions. They play upon them with insidious skill and expertise. Often with subtle and suggestive methods they fan the flames of bodily desires, until an inferno of passion for some product is aroused. It becomes an absolute priority in life. The place is reached where one simply *must have a luxury automobile—a mink stole—a mansion on the hill—a magnificent martini—an expensive cigarette—a Monaco holiday— a mistress—or any other of ten thousand tantalizing things.*

All or any one can so preoccupy us, can so monopolize us, that our view of God, our consciousness of Christ, our sense of His Spirit, is completely obstructed and distorted. Our communion is cut off. Our intimacy is impaired. Our harmony is fragmented. We no longer walk with Him in a clear, unclouded conscience. No longer are His desires our desires. No longer are His wishes our commands.

Instead we are consumed by our own desires.

3. *The World's Appeal to Our Vanity and Pride*

If we are intelligent and spiritually aware we will take a long, hard look at the techniques employed by the world to attract our attention. We will awaken to the realization that not only are we manipulated but actually exploited by the society of which we boast so proudly.

So much of the sophistication and expertise of modern man is aimed at the ego in all of us. The vanity and pride of our persons is appealed to with devastating impact.

We are told that we owe it to ourselves to own this or that. We are exhorted to pander to our passions. We are encouraged to impress others with our possessions. We are admonished to "get with it"; to live it up; to let go all restraints; to indulge every whim; to use all our powers; to express our own desires.

The cry of society is *"If it makes you feel good—then do it,"* no matter what the terrible consequences may be to you or to others around you whose lives are entwined with yours.

Increasingly the clarion call of the world is *"Do your own thing—go your own way—get all you can."*

By being approached through any one or all of our five bodily senses of sight, hearing, touch, taste, or smell, we are stimulated and excited to a life of total self-indulgence and self-gratification of our bodily desires, appetites, and passions.

Amid the fever and frenzy of following these fads, Christ comes to us as of old and calmly calls us by His Spirit:

If any man will come after me, let him deny himself, and take up his cross daily, and follow me.

For whosoever will save his life shall lose it: but whosoever will lose his life for my sake, the same shall save it.

For what is a man advantaged, if he gain the whole
world, and lose himself, or be cast away?

Luke 9:23–25

In a way this seems a bit absurd, a bit foolish, when
viewed against the glitter and glamour of the godless world
around us. For some it produces real, deep inner tension.
Which way really lies truth? What will I do with this body of
mine? Will I walk in the way of the world? Or will I follow
Christ in simplicity?

The Deception of Walking With the World

Our Lord was very emphatic about this matter. He put it
bluntly when He stated categorically:

No man can serve two masters; for either he will hate
one and love the other, or he will attach himself to one
and think lightly of the other. You cannot be servants
both of God and of money [or what money will buy].

Matthew 6:24 WEYMOUTH

This being the case, we should understand the reason for
the warning He gave about preoccupation with the gratifica-
tion of bodily desires through the use of material assets.

There are two: The first is one most of us forget. It is the
transient nature of all those things that titillate our bodily
desires. They are not permanent. They are not enduring.
They are not eternal values. If we build our lives around
them, we are building sand castles soon swept away in the
tides of time. They all come to *nothing*.

Absolutely inherent in the very nature of things that *seem to satisfy momentarily* is the inexorable process of decay.

Everything in the world is subject to change. All is in flux. Things deteriorate. Possessions depreciate. Health, vigor, beauty of body degenerate. All living organisms die. All possessions have a way of disappointing those who struggle to secure them. People discover that they do not own their things; their things own them, enslave them, bring them into bondage.

So if our sights are set only on such aims and ambitions, we have been deluded, deceived, and duped. We were made for greater good. We were made for God Himself. Anyone who settles for less than to honor Him, walk with Him, love Him, and serve Him, has shortchanged himself.

As God's people we are surrounded by a rising flood of worldly propaganda that appeals to our bodily desires. More and more we are caught up in it. Some are submerged in it. Some are being swept away with it. Dare we be different?

What Are You Using Your Body to Achieve?

Several months ago a young man sat in the shade of the trees on my lawn. He was only twenty-nine. He was keen, intelligent, enthusiastic, successful by the world's standards. He planned to retire the next year on his thirtieth birthday. The previous season his private business had exceeded $10 million. He drove a Cadillac. He flew the fastest turbojet in the country; he owned a beautiful ranch. He apparently "had it made."

In utter seriousness he looked me squarely in the eyes and said: "A person really does not want to come to the end of life's journey and find he hasn't really lived for anything eternal, enduring, or worthwhile!"

It was the most profound statement and serious thought he could entertain.

The questions that come to us are, "What am I doing with my body? What are its drives, its desires, its passions, its propensities being used for? Where am I going with it? Who am I walking with—the world or my God?"

Even that ancient sage Socrates made the astute observation centuries ago that *"he is nearest to God who has the fewest desires."*

Jesus Christ stated unashamedly and categorically, "A man's life simply does not consist in the abundance of things he possesses" (*see* Luke 12:15).

Not long ago, one of Hugh Hefner's so-called bunnies made a public statement that though she had become one of his favorite playmates, the whole performance was utterly phony. Here was someone who had been deluded to believe that her bodily desires could be fulfilled in glamour and gaiety. Instead she was totally disenchanted with its duplicity and deception. Sheer hypocrisy.

Where then does the secret to utter satisfaction lie?

Delight Yourself in the Lord

God's Word makes it very clear to us that He Himself, by His Spirit, resides in our bodies. They are called His temple, His habitation, His residence here on earth. (Read carefully through 1 Corinthians 6:12–20.)

In other words, both God and I are joint occupants of my body. We share the same premises. We cohabitate in the one residence. He is, therefore, my constant companion. An acute awareness of this will change my entire attitude toward the Lord.

There will begin to dawn upon my spirit and soul the *deep desire to delight in His companionship.* If we live together; love each other; respect each other; then surely we are bound to enjoy each other.

Too often there is a tendency to try and make this simple relationship between God and man too mystical; too mysterious; almost magical. It need not be.

How does one delight in God? Here are just a few simple suggestions. Use those same five physical senses of your body that the world exploits to intrude into your life, to make yourself aware, instead, of God.

Use your eyes to read His Word—to study it. Use them to revel in the sublime beauties of His creation around you.

Use your hearing to listen to the sounds of wind, waves, streams, bird song, the laughter of children, great music. Take your body where these can be found. Revel in them.

Use your sense of smell to inhale the fragrance of flowers, fresh earth after rain, ozone off the sea, hay curing in the sun, orchards in blossom. Thank Him for every perfume.

Use your taste buds to relish clear, cool water, delicious food, the delicacy of fresh fruit and vegetables. All come from Him.

Use your sense of touch to feel the smoothness of a rose, the roughness of tree bark, the warmth of sand between your toes, the luxuriance of grass and pine needles beneath your feet, the hand of your wife, husband, child, or sweetheart.

Every good and perfect gift comes to us in generous measure from our God. On every side He surrounds us with an overwhelming outpouring of His loving provision for our

bodily welfare. Submerge yourself in His generosity. Let an
upwelling stream of gratitude and delight pour from you in
ardent appreciation for His presence that surrounds you on
every side.

It is in Him that you live and move and have your very
being. And it is in you that He lives and moves and has His
very being. Become acutely, intensely aware of this interre-
lationship. Revel in Him. Rejoice in Him. Rest in Him.

It is He who will impart to you His own exquisite desires.
It is He who will impress upon you His own divine designs.
It is He who will consummate all of these as you share life
with Him, walking together in sincere, calm, quiet harmony.
Walking with God can be beautiful, beautiful, beautiful!

Trust in the Lord, and do good; so shalt thou dwell in
the land, and verily thou shalt be fed. Delight thyself
also in the Lord; and he shall give thee the desires of
thine heart.

Psalms 37:3, 4

Take Time to Be Absolutely Alone With God

As you become increasingly aware of God's presence in
your life, you will become increasingly fond of Him. You
will find that Christ really is your favorite Friend. You will
want to be alone in intimate communion.

One does not have to go into some closed room to do this.
Your special rendezvous can be anywhere, at any time, provided you take the trouble to deliberately go to your trysting
place.

Different people will have different ways of doing this.
Most of my precious moments with the Master are when I

take a walk outdoors alone or work in the garden or stroll by the sea. But by all means get alone; get quiet; get relaxed and allow Him to share some very private, precious moments with you.

Close out the clamor of the world all around.

Give Yourself Completely to God

In our hectic, hedonistic society, we give ourselves freely to every new fad or freakish thing that comes along. We give our energy, time, strength, and resources to searching, striving, and struggling to attain all sorts of transient things that tarnish with time.

Give yourself as enthusiastically to God! What powerful, potent people we would be if He really held prior place in our interests. Society would be startled and shaken if it could see men and women as much given to God as most are given to gold.

Really put Christ first. Consult Him about all of your interests and activities. Be acutely conscious that your bodily well-being and behavior affect Him as much as they do you. It will sober you up no end as to what you eat, what you drink, what you wear, where you go, how you behave. Get serious with God about your body. It is as much His residence as yours. Respect His rights in it. Put His requirements first. Recognize that He really owns it, not you, so you do have a responsibility to put His desires first.

As you do, you will discover that He, not the world around you, will become your preoccupation. You will be startled to see that your entire perspective on life alters. Your chief center of interest will shift from yourself to Him. The world, society, and all its selfish self-centeredness will begin to appear both absurd and vainly stupid. For the first time you will begin to have a balanced view of reality.

There will steal over you, as you walk with God in this way, the awareness that He brought you into being for Himself. You were made for Him. You can give yourself to nothing or no one greater. Knowing Him; loving Him; enjoying Him; serving Him; walking with Him, is the whole end and purpose of life.

As He becomes the center of your life, you will find that He in turn takes care of and satisfies all your other desires, appetites, and passions. (*See* Matthew 6:33.)

This is the explosive power of a newfound affection.

CHAPTER

3

Walking With God
in My Bodily Behavior

It should be obvious to the reader that if in fact we do actually walk with God in both our bodily drives and bodily desires, this should be reflected in our bodily behavior. Our daily life habits that concern our bodies will demonstrate beyond doubt that we are a unique people keeping company with God.

The foregoing is simple enough to say on paper or to express in pious pronouncements. It is a totally different thing to translate it into a superior, sensible life-style. As some of God's greatest saints have observed again and again across the centuries, "One of the most difficult and demanding things in all the world is to be a truly well-balanced Christian who reflects the Character of Christ in our daily conduct."

Godly Behavior Cannot Be Legislated

All through the history of the church the followers of Christ have tended to experience a certain tension between the rigid legalism of some sects and the extreme liberalism of others. Certain denominations have endeavored to establish arbitrary rules of conduct for their people which often lead to very strict and severe censure of all those who do not so conduct themselves.

Frequently a violent reaction has developed, especially among the young, against such legalism. Especially at times of spiritual renewal, some have allowed themselves to cast all restraint to the winds. They have, as Paul put it so forcefully, used their liberation of spirit to become an excuse for improper and inappropriate bodily behavior. Human beings are ever thus. We tend to swing erratically from one extreme of the pendulum of human conduct to the other.

> For, brethren, ye have been called unto liberty; only use not liberty for an occasion to the flesh, but by love serve one another. For all the law is fulfilled in one word, even in this; Thou shalt love thy neighbour as thyself.
>
> Galatians 5:13, 14

It is a well-known fact that human goodness and wholesome, godly behavior simply cannot be legislated. Commendable conduct cannot be imposed upon people from without. There must be an internal transformation of the inner springs of our desire to live holy, wholesome lives. This book has been an honest and sincere endeavor to show how that can and does happen in spirit, soul, and body.

But when all has been said and done, there still must be some specific, definite guidelines as to how we do walk with God in our bodily behavior. Happily for us they are available. We have not been left in the dark. There are two powerful principles which should always govern our daily habits.

Two Powerful Principles That Determine Our Bodily Behavior

1) The first of these is the one which has been discussed over and over again in this book: *My bodily needs, their drives, and their desires are not to become the overriding priorities in life.*

The world all around me may so live. But not I. For me to live means putting God in Christ at the center of my conduct. Society, my culture, the media, my friends and family may all consider me a fool to seek God's interests first, above my own. Let them. God's Word to me is that if He occupies prior place in my conduct, He, too, can and will provide for my bodily requirements. He knows precisely what is best and will see that it is available.

2) The second great principle has likewise been given our attention in the preceding pages: My body is not just my own. It belongs to God as well. It is shared with Him. We are joint occupants in a shared residence. I do not, therefore, have the privilege to do as only I wish with my body.

I consult with Christ as to my conduct and daily habits. I live to bless and honor Him and benefit others. This is to walk and move with Him in wholesome goodwill and happy harmony.

The Practical Application of the First Principle

If in quiet, sincere, unostentatious cooperation with God's Spirit I set myself to put God first, then I shall not allow myself to become:

A food faddist
A drink addict
A health nut or physical-fitness freak
A workaholic
A pursuer of pleasure and leisure
A vain dresser
A sexual pervert
A pill pusher or drug addict

The reasons for this should be very obvious to the reader. Undue preoccupation with any of these behavior patterns immediately usurps the place of God in my life. For my god is that to which I devote most of my time, strength, and attention. And tragically for all of us, any one of the above pursuits can readily become the very hub and center about which all of our bodily habits revolve.

Second, we simply must see that if we succumb to the subtle suggestions and blatant blandishments of the world around us we can readily become preoccupied with any one or all of these pursuits. Books, pamphlets, programs, and propaganda of a thousand sorts would lead us to believe that we owe it to ourselves to become submerged in this sort of behavior. We do not.

We dare not ever allow any of them to intrude themselves between us and God. They must never divert or deflect our attention from being fastened on Him whom to know is life and health and well-being.

It is true that we have an obligation to Him and to ourselves to keep our bodies fit, well, energetic, and wholesome. How then do we proceed? By applying the second principle to each area of our bodily behavior.

The Simple, Practical Application of the Second Principle

As it becomes increasingly apparent to me that my body has been entrusted to me by God as a serious responsibility, I shall care for it with a new view. I shall see it no longer as my sole property. Rather it will be regarded as a shared estate whose maintenance in good order is up to me.

Put in rather simple but understandable terms, it can be said that the Master is in residence, and I am the grounds keeper. Together we share the premises. Together we benefit from His ownership and my caretaking activities. Together we both live and walk in and enjoy its occupancy. Whoever else may enter or touch this residence will be refreshed and benefited by the encounter. This body of mine is both God's home and my home for the few short years we share its occupancy.

Here, then, are some basic patterns of balanced behavior for my body. The following are but the bare outline.

The body in which God and I reside and walk.

It is a beautiful body! Not necessarily a glamorous, slick, Hollywood-handsome body, but a body of beautiful design and exquisite craftsmanship.

It has the remarkable capacity for growth. It can reproduce itself. It has the incredible ability to automatically resist and repulse the invasion of disease organisms. It can heal itself, given proper care and nourishment. It can replenish and renew itself year after year.

The body has the capacity to adapt itself to enormous climate changes; to various nutritional diets; to diverse cultural patterns of life. It can withstand enormous stress and strain, yet still survive for well nigh a hundred years.

Because it is a beautiful organism of divine design it deserves my utmost respect; it deserves proper care; it deserves dignity. It is not mine to abuse or misuse.

At one time it was common in the church to consider the body as almost abhorrent and essentially evil. It is not. It is God's gift to us as our earth house for our few years here. Let us treat it with gentle respect and gracious goodwill. (Read 1 Corinthians 6:12–20.)

Outdoor benefits for the body.

Not only did our Heavenly Father design our body but He also created the unique environment of planet earth to support and sustain it. The body enjoys life only so long as it is capable of correspondence with its environment. It was designed to derive its sustenance and energy from its surroundings.

Such beneficial environmental resources as sunlight, fresh air, clean water, warmth, nourishing food, and opportunities for recreation and relaxation are essential to bodily well-being.

Therefore, you as a person have a very serious obligation both to God and to yourself to expose your body to the environmental benefits that are available. You should see to it that you get out into the fresh air, the sunshine, the beautiful, natural surroundings of the wondrous outdoor world our Father has provided for our well-being. Get out and walk briskly. Commune quietly with Christ. Speak to His Spirit within you. Let Him speak to you.

Thank Him for sunshine, clouds, rain, mist, dew, leaves,

grass, earth, trees, flowers, shrubs, hills, plains, fields, forests, birds, animals, butterflies, streams, oceans, lakes, rocks, sand, soil, and ten thousand other sights, sounds, and smells that enliven your body and inspire your soul.

He surrounds you on every side with evidence of His thought, care, love, and provision for your well-being. Be glad in Him. Rejoice in His company. Relish His presence. Reflect on His infinite resources that invigorate and energize your body. Let gratitude to Him engulf your whole being. (Read Psalms 19:1–5.)

Bodily exercise.

It is recognized that more and more people are living in gigantic metropolitan areas. The opportunities for outdoor living and outdoor enjoyment are much fewer for the city person than for the country resident. Still there are parks and playgrounds; strips of beach or river front; open spaces here and there where the earth is not yet completely covered with concrete or asphalt.

Avail yourself of these. If need be, seek the sunshine and fresh air, if not unduly polluted, on a backyard lawn or open rooftop. Take brisk walks or short runs to exercise your body and fill your lungs with great drafts of fresh, oxygen-charged air. Drive less and walk more.

On days off seek the seclusion of some quiet countryside where you can swim in the sea or lake or stream. Take a walk in the woods. Climb a hill or track a bird or an animal in the snow. Let the songs of birds and wind and waves wash over your weary body. Let the caress of sunshine, mist, and balmy breezes touch your bare cheeks, arms, and legs.

If you are one who needs some special stimulus to take

you outdoors for exercise become a rock hound; bird-watcher; shell collecter or tree specialist; wild-flower photographer; camping enthusiast; home gardener. There are endless outdoor interests which will enrich your life, provide plenty of exercise, and benefit your body.

All of these will each, in its own wondrous way, help you to become a beautiful, balanced person charged with enthusiasm and bodily vigor.

Amid any or all of these activities, give God thanks for the good gifts which He has bestowed upon you out of the bounty of His beautiful, natural world. Thank Him humbly for bodily strength, stamina, and senses that enable you to interact so exquisitely with the wondrous environment all around you. (Read Acts 17:24–31.)

Bodily rest and relaxation.

If a person is consistent in seeing to it that he does get some outdoor activity, it is not likely he will have any difficulty with proper rest or sleep. The body, refreshed yet weary and contented, quickly slips into sweet and gentle slumber.

It is part and parcel of God's amazing provision for us that our bodies should have regular rest and relaxation. We simply were not designed to work day and night without letup. Those who boast brashly that they would rather "wear out than rust out" are hardly wise. Even God Himself rested after His great creative enterprises. Our Lord, while here as a man, slipped away quietly from the crowds so as to be alone; to rest, to relax; to commune quietly with His Father.

God has arranged that man should spend at least one day

in seven in quiet, untroubled rest and gentle relaxation for the restoration of his bodily vigor. We ignore this regime at our own peril. Only a fool will push himself relentlessly without letup and boast of his behavior.

Arrange your day and night so that you do get quiet, regular, restful sleep. Select and purchase a firm mattress that insures proper bodily support and sound sleep. If need be, take a midday siesta to rejuvenate yourself, especially if your days are long and nights short.

Surprising as it may seem, often it is during our times of rest that God takes the opportunity to speak most clearly and distinctly to us. For a short time our feverish activities are stilled. Then it is we best hear His Spirit's still, small voice saying to us, "This is the way—walk in it." (Read Psalms 4 and 127.)

Bodily labor and work.

Work is not a dirty word. Labor is not evil. There can be great dignity, intense creativity, enormous pleasure in work well done. It matters not whether it is digging a garden, building a home, baking bread, or writing a book. Don't overdo it, but enjoy it.

Work is one of God's greatest gifts to His people. It need not be something we shun or shirk. Scripture is abundantly clear that we should work diligently, energetically, and with enthusiasm (en-Theo—IN-GOD) at whatever we do.

His name, His reputation, His honor are as much at stake in the project as is mine. Whatever I find to do, therefore, I will employ all my bodily resources to accomplish in the very finest performance possible.

The secret to joyous work is to recognize that God and I are co-workers. It is a shared project. He is in it with me. Together we will turn out the best possible product.

I never put my pen to the paper (all my books are handwritten in long-hand, using an old-fashioned fountain pen) without first consciously, sincerely consulting with Christ about what will be written and in what manner.

The net result is that one need not take personal, selfish pride in the final product. It has been a joint effort in which He is the senior partner and prime consultant. Such bodily work is beautiful; it is upbuilding and deeply gratifying. (Read Colossians 3:22–24; 2 Thessalonians 3:8–16.)

Bodily food: eating.

Eat only as much as you need. No more! The Arabs have a marvelous saying: "Enough is a feast." Most of us in the Western world eat far too much, too often.

Eat regularly, but sparingly. Keep fit, keep trim. We are not to be gluttons.

Get up early enough to eat a proper breakfast of nourishing food. Your body must be fortified to function efficiently throughout the day. You do yourself, and God, great disservice by crawling through the day on little more than a cup of coffee or a single slice of sickly toast.

Eat regular meals of wholesome foods. Avoid processed and refined products that have been robbed of their nutritious elements. Insure that your diet is rich in fresh vegetables, fresh fruits, fresh dairy products, and fresh meats.

Simply refuse to bludgeon and abuse your beautiful body with junk foods, fancy pastries, caustic condiments, excess salt, pickles, or preserved fruits that are afloat in white sugar.

Eat plenty of roughage. Eat simply. Eat in a cheerful atmosphere, with genuine gratitude for every good and wholesome dish you relish—it is a gift from God. (Read Matthew
6:24–34.)

Bodily thirst: drinking.

The body is approximately 70 percent moisture. The liq-
uids essential to health and bodily well-being must be continually replenished. Clean, clear water is adequate.

Culture and society demand the brewing and drinking of
beverages. If you are hopelessly addicted to coffee or tea
with their stimulants of caffeine or tannin, do not point the
finger of reproach at the alcoholic addicted to his or her
drink.

Whatever you drink, apart from water, milk, or fresh fruit
juices should be in the utmost moderation. You have no
right to abuse God's residence with brews or concoctions
that will complicate your life and do damage to your body.

Our stimulation should come from God's own gracious
Spirit, not from some spurious spirits out of a bottle or pot.

The Word of God is very clear, very specific in this area.
We are not to allow our society, our culture, or our associates to compress us into the mold of their life-style. Any
drink, no matter how sociable it may seem, should not be
indulged in if it damages or debilitates the body.

In all areas of eating, drinking, and bodily behavior we
are told explicitly to walk with God in great consciousness
and careful moderation. (Read Ephesians 5:14–20.)

Bodily medication and drug usage.

The body, if properly fed, nourished, exercised, rested,
and exposed to outdoor benefits, has an enormous capacity

to continue in good health. It can repel disease, heal itself, and function freely with an absolute minimum of medication.

Of course there can be accidents, emergencies, and desperate diseases which demand the service of medical science to assist in its recovery. But the body need not become dependent on and addicted to medications, stimulants, or sedatives. It was never so intended.

We do not have to rely on pills and prescriptions to pull us through life. We can, if we so choose, and so determine with God's help, be wholesome in body, fit, well and able to serve Him acceptably. Some of us, with simple, quiet, trusting faith in God have found across the years He can make us whole. He can renew our strength. He can keep us in health to do His work in the world.

It is significant that in most of the recorded cases in which Jesus healed the sick, He first asked what they really wanted. Did they really will to be well? Did they really desire to be delivered? Wanting to be well and whole and holy for God's residence is halfway to becoming healthy in body.

Merely in passing, let it be said that no person wanting to walk with God in his body will ever indulge in drug addiction such as LSD, marijuana, cocaine, or heroin. These are ultimately destructive. They have no place in the Christian's bodily behavior. (Read James 5; 1 Peter 1:13–21.)

Bodily sexual behavior.

As I have said before, numerous books, pamphlets, articles, and programs proliferate on this subject. It cannot possibly be discussed here in detail.

Bodily sexual activity, within the framework of a Christian home, in loyal, faithful commitment to a true life mate can be beautiful, beautiful, beautiful.

Regular, joyous, gracious self-giving relaxes the participants; energizes the body; beautifies its appearance, and enhances its vigor and vitality.

As with eating, so with sex: *"Enough is a feast."* We are not to become involved in sexual perversion that leads to lust, licentiousness, fornication, adultery, cruelty, sadism, or masochism.

It is a beautiful, wondrous, exhilarating, and beneficial bodily function designed by God. Cherish it and be grateful for so great a gift. Keep your bodily behavior in this realm wholesome, clean, and uncontaminated by the crude culture of your day.

Those who sell their bodies cheap for kicks in sex will live to rue the day and kick themselves for their own folly! (Read Colossians 3:1–15; 2 Peter 2:1–22.)

Conclusion

The preceding pages have been an honest attempt to give you, the reader, practical, helpful guidance in your bodily behavior as you walk with God. Never forget the Master is ever with you. He can be your dearest Friend, your most intimate Associate. His gracious Spirit, who resides in you, can be your closest Confidante, your constant Companion, your Counselor.

Learn to walk with Him in joy, devotion, and dignity.

Do Him the great honor of walking with Him in quiet, happy harmony—a child of His!

HEADING HOME

Oh, God, my Heavenly Father,
        my constant Friend,
                my joyous Fellow on the path of life,
It is wonderful to know Your voice.
    It is heartening to sense Your hand.
        It is thrilling to enjoy Your company.
Thank You for sharing the tough trails of life
    with this wayfarer heading home.